Testimon.....

Betty Walker and *"To Keep or Not To Keep"* . . .

"To Keep or Not To Keep" is a valuable collection of stories for those considering abortions, those who have already had them, and for their families. It opens our eyes to the far-reaching trauma associated with the lies behind this so-called "quick-fix." Within these pages, we find the grace to step into the future with fresh hope and healing from the Deliverer whose love never fails.

Cheryl Ricker,
Author of *"A Friend in the Storm"*
and *"Rush of Heaven"*

In this book, Betty Walker opens our eyes both to a hidden world of pain and consequences surrounding the act of abortion and to the loving work of Christ that heals and frees. From her experience in listening, counseling and praying with individuals, your sensitivity will expand and so will your hope. The book is worth a thoughtful read and is especially helpful to families confronted with either a history of abortion or a recommendation to have one.

The Rev. Dr. Wesley J. Gabel,
Pastor of Grace United Methodist Church
Fergus Falls, MN

Betty and her husband Bob consistently communicate with women who have had an abortion. She knows the brokenness that invariably follows abortions. Betty compassionately offers help and hope in a godly manner for those responding to post abortion experiences. "To Keep or Not to Keep" is about God's grace that truly is amazing.

Wendell Amstutz, Author,
President of National Community Resource Center

It's wrong.
It's a sin.
It's murder.
It's a choice.
It's a clump of cells.

Call "it" what you will, IT is the very beginning of a human life, made and created by the only one who can give breath to a living being. This book, so eloquently and gently written from the loving heart of Betty Walker, was born out of a deep desire to help others see what abortion truly is; the intentional ending of a human life. The testimonies inside are not meant for guilt, fear or manipulation. This book is about what happens when we let our society tell us what is okay, justifying our actions and allowing ourselves to do what is legal because it will "solve" a temporary "problem". But the choice of abortion is never temporary. If you get nothing else out of this book, I hope you read these words: FORGIVENESS IS A GIFT WE ALL CAN RECEIVE. Thank you, Betty (and all those who've shared their stories) for putting your heart and soul into the pages of this book.

Betsy Singer,
TV Anchor/Reporter

As a woman in ministry for many years, I have prayed with women over and over who are wrestling with some of the choices they have made in life. Abortion is an issue that affects women profoundly, adversely, and deeply. Thank you, Betty, for this straightforward and loving sharing of women's stories and experiences, all wrapped in the hope and healing that is available to us because of Jesus.

Pastor Kristi Graner,
Founder and Director of Dare to Believe Ministries

This is a compelling and very deeply spiritual analysis of the abortion issue with scripture references and personal accounts of individuals who have experienced abortion and its lasting effects on their lives. I would highly recommend this to everyone no matter what side of the issue you are currently on.

Casey Caldwell M.D.

TO KEEP OR NOT TO KEEP

A spiritual book on abortion

by

Betty Walker

With love and blessings,
Betty Walker

To Keep or Not To Keep by Betty Walker

Published by GDI (Graphic Design, Inc.)
315 Second Street East
Hastings, Minnesota 55033-0307
www.gd-inc.com

Cover design by Howard Lower
Production assistance by Bev Lower
Lower Photography & Studio, Rochester, MN
www.lowerphotography.com

Edited by Tom and Kathy Pouk

International Standard Book Number (ISBN): 978-0-692-48607-8

First edition

Visit author's website at www.jonathanhouseministries.com

ACKNOWLEDGMENTS

It's said that it takes a village to raise a child. It could also be said it takes a village to write a book. Like with every other book I have written, it takes many hands working together to arrive at the finish line. To all of the dedicated folks who worked tirelessly contributing to the success of this project and expect nothing in return I say "THANK YOU!" Day-after-day they have shared their God-given gifts and talents, and consistently delivered more than what was asked or expected. These people are rare jewels!

Howard and Bev Lower, founders of Lower Photography & Studio, have gone beyond incredible throughout the entire process of writing this book. Thank you, Howard, for your creativity in designing the book cover, as well as your attention to detail. Bev, you truly are a friend that sticks closer than a brother (sister). Your steadfast commitment to help me sort out the handwritten chapters, look up numerous scriptures, and tireless research is greatly appreciated. Thank you for bringing such strength and encouragement throughout this project. It is with sincere praise and a full heart that I say, "Thank you. May God richly bless you both and reward you for a job well done."

To Paula, Kathy, Stephanie, and Kurt, thank you so much for sharing your stories with the world. I admire your courage and determination to let your voices be heard. All of you are such an encouragement and inspiration to observe how you have allowed God to take a painful experience in your life and bring about glory and praise for Him. Keep sharing your stories; they are making a difference.

Tom and Kathy Pouk, words cannot express the gratitude I have for all of your support and help during this project. Thank you for the countless hours you have selflessly given combing over the details and working to resolve the behind the scenes issues that arise during a project such as this. You two are truly a God-send. Thank you again for modeling what true servanthood should look like. May God abundantly bless both of you.

Blessings,
Betty

CONTENTS

FOREWORD

"What difference does it make anyway?"

These are the words that I heard from a person asking me the question "Why is the abortion topic such a big issue?"

When I was a child, I don't think I ever heard any adult even talk about the topic of abortion. In fact, as a kid I didn't even know what the word meant!

Yet, we all know about the Roe vs. Wade landmark decision by the United States Supreme Court back in 1973 that redefined the rights of a woman and allowed abortion to become legal.

In 1973, I was only ten years old. Not until high school did I recall hearing much about this major decision except in my health class.

Yet at the age of 30, I had just been voted in as the lead pastor of a dynamic church in Seattle, Washington, my eyes and my heart would be forever changed! I still recall having a person come to my office wanting to discuss the topic of abortion with me. They had brought with them some videos of an actual abortion and the process that took place in eliminating a baby. As I sat in one of our Sunday school classrooms watching the video, I was in shock! First of all, I could not believe that they would videotape this and show it to people like me. And secondly, I couldn't believe that someone would ever want to take the life of one of these little babies created in the image of God!

Let's just say that from that day until now, I have never been the same. I didn't realize the impact that abortion had on the mother and even the father. I have watched grown men sob uncontrollably as they relived the fact that they took the life of their child and will never be able to see them grow up! I have watched mothers who aborted their child, unable to function in society because every day they wonder if God will forgive them for taking the life of their unborn child!

As a pastor, I know that this is a huge topic in the church and everyone has an opinion. The author of this book has an opinion as well. Not because she personally has had an abortion, but because God has put this issue within her heart as she works with those wounded by their choices, who then come to The Jonathan House Ministries for help.

I encourage you to allow these stories to speak to you. Who knows, it could change your life and it could save the life of someone just like you.

Pastor Jim Filbeck
Rochester Assembly of God Church

Cover Story
I Kept Mine

I want you to know a little about my background. By the time I was a junior in high school, I had only seen my dad three or four times in my life. My mom partied in clubs while I took care of myself and my siblings. I did not feel love, or structure, or discipline in my life. As I matured, I rebelled by not going home when I should. I was "running my own show." I had no guidance from either parent. I knew the Lord, but I didn't have a good support system to help enhance my knowledge and spiritual growth.

There came a day when there was too much time between my monthly cycles, so I took a pregnancy test. "No, I can't be pregnant!" Then, "God, no!" it was positive the first time I tested! It was positive that day!

Shock took over! "I guess it's possible." So, I took the test again! It was positive. I was pregnant.

I went to New Life Family Services in Rochester, Minnesota, because I knew they would have a "better" pregnancy test. Once more – Positive! They offered me an ultrasound.

I heard the baby's heartbeat that very day!

They said the baby was about one month old. After they gave me all the options, they asked, "Do you want an abortion? We can recommend someone." My immediate response was, "No! I'm keeping it." They retorted "That's okay."

I knew that telling my mom would be the hardest thing to do, so I didn't go to her first. After all the only time she had commented about pregnancy was when she said to me, "If you ever get pregnant, don't come home."

I talked to my boyfriend's mom first. I was there talking for quite a while. She was very happy and so supportive. I told her that I didn't know what to say to my mom. She responded that it was getting late and my mom would be worried about me and where I might be.

I decided to send a Facebook message to my mom, saying "I'm pregnant." Mom's message back was, "What are you going to do? Keep it?" I replied, "Yes, I'm keeping it." I never felt my mother had any authority in my life and even though it was chaotic, I went home because at least there was some sense of love there.

My older brother became the most negative person in my life. He did not like the fact that I was pregnant! He was loud and hurtful. He messaged me on Facebook and said, "I know a clinic where you can get a free abortion. Are you set on your decision?" He called me names no one should use; let alone my older brother! His words wounded me deeply.

For me though, sex outside of marriage was the bigger issue. Losing my virginity was far worse than being pregnant because in 8th grade I had accepted Jesus as my savior and invited the Holy Spirit inside of me. "Jesus doesn't love me!" How that thought dug deep into my spirit. I had to keep that thought well-hidden, even from me so I wouldn't keep thinking about it. I did want to be married and thought I could never obtain it because the guilt over my sexual sin was so engulfing my spirit. But then I learned that with confession, repentance, and forgiveness (of myself and of others), through God's grace, there is total forgiveness!

My relationship with my boyfriend (my baby's father), was rocky. There I was pregnant, and he was entering Teen Challenge in the Twin Cities of Minnesota. I told him on my first visit. We had already broken up. After all, he had to take care of himself and his issues. As I presented the news, his quick response was, "You want to be my girlfriend?" Now being in that relationship we were able to sit and talk in a more private room together. He was excited and supportive. Since he was living in the Twin Cities, I could only visit one time a month. I had just finished with my junior year in high school, was starting my senior year, working, and having a baby. Visiting once a month was all I could accomplish.

Back home, things were getting horribly cruel between my older brother and me. When I was three to four months pregnant, we got into a physical confrontation and during it he hit me on my stomach. He was argumentative and disgusted with me. My mom knew it was happening, but did nothing. She did not stand against his actions. I could not take my brother's abusive behavior, so I moved out.

I thought I was following God, but since I set such a bad example, I felt I was a failure, and a hypocrite! I was alone. I battled without family support. I believed in God, but the enemy was kicking me!

Then an elderly woman, who I call Berg, offered me a place to stay that very day! We lived together until I could get my own apartment. Berg talked about God a great deal. Now with a new friend, Berg, I found myself participating in Bible studies with a group who cared. I also helped her a bit when I could. It was a blessed time for us both.

One day while I was lying on my bed, I fell in love with God. God the Father wrapped His arms around me. He held me. I have had other experiences of God's presence and great love. But that day, as He held me, He just stayed there, holding me. Holding me like my daddy should have done. He was everything to me that day.

He gave me a new perspective. He was EVERYTHING to me! And it was better than I wanted or expected, causing me to seek Him even more.

I had an amazing pregnancy as God was constantly with me, and still is. His gift of the life of my baby boy has been remarkable! I totally love them both.

Deuteronomy 30:19-21 (ESV)
I call heaven and earth as witnesses today against you, that I have set before you life and death, blessing and cursing; therefore choose life, that both you and your descendants may live; that you may love the LORD your God, that you may obey His voice, and that you may cling to Him, for He is your life and the length of your days; and that you may dwell in the land which the LORD swore to your fathers, to Abraham, Isaac, and Jacob, to give them.

To Keep or Not To Keep

Preface
Listen

It is extremely difficult to know where and how to enter into this journey that the Lord has put upon my heart to write this book. At The Jonathon House, we minister with so many hurting people that it makes my heart heavy, but I tend not to dwell on such things so that it will not bring me down or dampen my spirit!

Soon after moving to Rochester, Minnesota, in 2001, the Lord led us to establish The Jonathan House Ministries where we have been in Christian ministry ever since. It has been, and still is from time-to-time, a rocky road. Nevertheless, we have seen substantial transformation in people's lives! It still astonishes us. We have observed countless numbers of people with such heavy loads of pain, guilt, and sin, as well as other heaviness, that it is totally incredible how they function!

It is staggering to contemplate how many innocent babies have been murdered because of a bad or poor choice. We don't need to attempt to hide or erase our poor choices, but bring them before the Lord Jesus and ask for forgiveness, and then go forward in what the Lord tells us to do. In spite of a poor choice, He will lead us in the right path to bring glory to Him. Please listen to His voice when He speaks to you!

In each of the chapters that follow are the stories of various individuals. Some are men, others are women. Some aborted their babies, while others chose to give their baby up for adoption, or to go on and parent their child. There is even the story of a godly man who survived multiple attempts on his life even before coming forth from his mother's womb.

In every case, God is the one who removes the hurt and replaces it with love, forgiveness, and a life of liberty. Then, He authorizes us to serve Him in remarkable ways.

I pray that you will receive what I have to share within these pages! Let Him prepare your way.

Blessings,
Betty Walker

Introduction
Would You Murder Your Baby?

I cannot begin to express what I feel within my spirit concerning abortion! I have always known it was very wrong, but in my innocence, I never thought deeply about abortion. I grew up in a Christian home and went to church every time the doors were open. On both sides of my family, everyone was a member of the Methodist Church. (Please understand that in what I am going to say, I am not coming against the Methodist Church. I know there are lots of people in those churches who really love the Lord and serve Him.) My father was the praise leader in our church and I began to play the piano at church while I was in early grade school. I really enjoyed doing that! It gave me a feeling of significance which was important to me at that time.

On both sides of our family, divorce and other such things were not evident; they all were very clean, decent people who were in church for all functions. My uncle taught a Sunday school class in our church for all my childhood years. We worked hard and did all the things that we thought were good, pure, and holy. Worldly things were not discussed in our family; we just did all the right things. Of course, back then abortion was never mentioned and probably not done – as I was born in 1935. Because I didn't have deep discussions with my parents about worldly issues, I was very innocent about lots of things and had to learn on my own as I grew up. I tried very hard to follow in their footsteps.

My husband, Bobby, and I married when we were 17. I had a year and a half left to finish high school and did well in school, graduating with the rest of my class. We were married six years before we started our family. We always wanted a family, but because we were so young, we decided to wait. Praise God that He allowed it to be that way! It was very evident that the Lord was in control of our lives in that when our children did come, He gave me the strength to get each one potty-trained, and out of diapers at least a month before the next one arrived.

It wasn't until the Lord began to really bring us into a deeper relationship with Him that lots of issues became clear to me. We were led to a Spirit-filled, non-denominational church later in life and began to learn so much about Him and living even more for Him. It truly changed our lives and blessed us abundantly. Then later, we moved back to Texas to assist my aging parents and again the Lord led us to a Spirit-filled church that taught us about spiritual warfare and deliverance. Believe me, it really opened our eyes. We learned about things we had never thought about before. Before moving back to Texas, I saw our grandson, Jonathan, healed of epilepsy in an elevator on the way to a brain scan. Jonathan had been ill with seizures for a little over four years, and the Lord healed him through prayer and fasting. The complete story of this is in my book, *Trust Me, Child!*

After my parents died, and because I had developed several physical problems, we moved to Rochester, Minnesota, where our daughter and her family lived and it also was where the Mayo Clinic was. Subsequently, we established The Jonathan House Ministries, a healing and deliverance ministry. We have since worked with hundreds of people. Believe me, we have seen just about everything in people's lives. The baggage people carry is amazing. Matters from their past, their parent's and grandparent's past, physical, mental, and spiritual issues from experiences with family and other individuals are astounding.

Needless to say, we have worked with many women who have had abortions and worked with some men who didn't know until after it was over. Lots of women to whom we have ministered have had at least three or four abortions! That statement is difficult for me to believe; but it is true! We have witnessed wonderful healings, both emotional and physical, during or soon after they went through deliverance. During the process of deliverance, they confess, repent, and forgive themselves and others, and receive freedom and healing from God. Following their session, we teach them how to walk in their new-found freedom!

A couple of years ago, I was driving down a street here in Rochester and a large billboard caught my eye. It was a beautiful picture of a newborn baby with huge printing over the picture stating, "Would you murder this baby?" I cannot explain how seeing the word *murder* on that image crushed me. I guess, in my innocence, I could not comprehend that people – especially Christian people – would do that to an unborn child. How could they do that to God's creation? It was at that point that I knew I had to bring this situation about abortion to the forefront because God's people, and even people who do not yet know Him, need to understand the complications and consequences that come as a result of the decisions that they make.

Shortly thereafter, at church during Sanctity of Life week (which is a week that is set aside to educate God's people about abortion), our pastor, Jim Filbeck had a member of his staff, a young woman, Paula, give her testimony to the congregation about having had an abortion when she was younger. The way she presented her life story really touched me – not unlike the billboard had. I felt like the Lord said, "Betty, you need to write a book about all these things to bring forth the importance of what is going on in so many lives." It genuinely touched my heart, but I was already in the process of writing another book; *God's Flower Garden*, so I knew it would have to wait.

Then, the following year, when again Paula gave her testimony at church, it was as if the Lord said to me, "Are you going to do this or not? This is the last time I am going to ask you to do this!" I replied, "Yes, Lord. I will do this and will start it this year."

I pray that the testimonies and teachings contained in this book will touch your life inspiring you to be able to speak freely about how these horrible events are affecting our families because so many beautiful, innocent babies are being murdered every day in our own communities and around the world.

Several potent narratives are included that will witness to you as to what our Lord can do. Even if and when you make bad decisions, God is with you. I anticipate that these journals of consequences and records of victories will speak to your heart. As they do, I would encourage you to communicate them to your family, friends, and others you know who might be in the process of considering ending the life of an unborn, precious child! A tiny one who will not have the opportunity to experience life because it was ended before they had a chance to blossom like our Lord intended for them. Though they were destined for His glory, they no longer exist!

I can imagine how making better choices about a baby's life will help your spirit reach new heights. I also know how deliverance brings healing to the spirit, soul, and body of someone who made the decision to abort.

For this reason I have included the testimonies of women who have decided not to abort, regardless of what it does to their lives and reputation. Their resolve was to give birth to children that God created, no matter their situation. I pray this speaks to your heart and to the hearts of your families and friends. We begin with Paula's story.

Chapter 1
Broken Chains

"It's okay! You're almost all back to normal now!"

Her words hung heavy in my thoughts. They echoed over and over in my mind like a broken record; following me like a shadow that I could never escape. The tone of her voice seemed to suggest that just moments before, I was somehow abnormal.

I tried to escape the memory of the touch of her hand on my right shoulder. She lightly gripped and then patted it, as though she were reassuring me to not doubt or second guess what had just been done – what I had done; what we all had done together. But it was to no avail. If anything, the memory of that which had just been executed with her help and with the assistance of a man dressed in a white lab coat only got stronger.

I remember him walking into the room, and sitting down on a stool at the end of the procedure table. I found myself taking notice that his hair was covered. I guess I was trying to distract my thoughts of how completely awkward and exposed I felt in his presence. His eyes and forehead were the only things I ever focused on as I lay on that cold table, looking over my bent knees that had been draped with a white sheet. He gave no formal introduction. He never even mentioned his name. He offered no personal care, no words. Not even a handshake. Yet with that man I made a horrible agreement that was to become the worst decision of my life. He was in the room, and then gone, in what seemed only a matter of minutes.

Why did I place such trust in these people who I had never met until that moment? I guess I was so scared that I thought I had no other choice. At that time in my life, fear had such a strong grip on me. Fear eventually bound me up like a chain that link by link wrapped itself tightly around me. Fear was certainly a primary factor in the choice that I had just made.

I remember the torment of such thoughts as, "What will people think of you?" "You aren't ready for this responsibility; it will ruin your life." "Paula, this is a mistake. Just take care of it and nobody will ever need to know." "Everyone will be disappointed in you and you won't be able to live your life how you want to."

I guess, somehow, in my naivety and pride, I justified my decision and decided I could just secretly take care of "it" and then forget about "it" forever. But instead, contrary to what I desired and thought would happen, that day was forever tattooed on my heart. February 19th, 1994 was the day my child went to be with the Lord because of my choice. It was on that day, due to my choice and due to the choices of the abortionist and the woman who assisted him by participating in that gruesome act, that a great divide came between me and God. What I didn't realize then, and know much too well now, was how much I would suffer silently for years. Because of that choice, and the series of choices I had made leading up to that juncture, I figured that I had gone too far and was unforgiveable.

Oh, what I would give, if I could just go back and tell my 18 year old self how foolish and deceived I was, and that the destructive lifestyle I was carelessly living was the wrong way! I was so lost. I was just desperately seeking to fill a void that no person could ever fill, nor was even meant to fill. If I could just tell that younger me to think about someone other than just myself for once, maybe things would have turned out differently.

To this day, I try not to remember the pain and tugging sensation I felt during the "procedure." But that is just something you can't forget no matter how much you try. The sound of the suction machine, and images of my aborted child, have since cried out and tormented me in my dreams at night.

When that lady at the facility told me, "It's okay! You're almost all back to normal now." I wanted to believe her. For a long while, I did. Her actions and words portrayed that she was helping me, but in the long run, they were really just a detriment to my well-being.

I can't help but wonder how many other young girls were told this very same thing! I wonder if that lady had to tell herself that same lie every time she assisted in the "procedures." Once we are able to talk ourselves into believing the lies, we fool our conscience, making our deeds that much easier.

That Saturday morning as I lay on the procedure table, staring at the white ceiling, one single warm tear slowly rolled down my right cheek. In that moment I replied back to her and said, "THANK GOD!" Who says that? Well, I did...a broken and fearful person who didn't truly know God, the creator of life, or His Son, Jesus Christ. I am certain now, decades later that MY God was not pleased with any of our choices.

Ten to fifteen girls just like me were sitting in the waiting room, waiting for their name to be called and then to be taken back to the procedure room. If those stale white waiting room walls could talk, I wonder what stories they could tell about the lives that were drastically changed within their confines!

The father of my baby sat in that waiting room – waiting while his child's life came to an end. How many children died that day? And how many people were forever changed at that facility on February 19th, 1994?

Abortion. That's what we call this act that we justify. It is nothing but destruction in so many ways. That deadly procedure did not undo the fact that I was still a mother. Abortion just made me the mother of a child who had been murdered with my consent. I actually paid them just a little over $300 to end the life that was growing inside of me. "No big deal, it's just a clump of cells, just a mass of tissue," they told me. If it was no big deal, then why does it hurt so deep within my heart? It sickens me to my very core to even have to process that reality. Even though I have dared to work through the healing process decades later, as I was sitting on my couch writing out my testimony, my chest tightened, I could barely breathe and my hand instinctively cupped my mouth in disbelief, disgust, anger and heartache at the realization of the person I was and what I did.

What seemed that day to be a simple transaction, ended up being a very complicated reality that haunted me for years. For $300, I got rid of what I now know to be one of the greatest gifts the Good Lord could ever give! I didn't realize that payment for "services" was just the beginning of a series of hardships, addictions, risky behaviors, torment, shame, guilt, low self-worth, and nightmares. Millions of silent tears fell from my shattered heart that eventually hardened and turned cold. There are dozens of unanswered questions and wonders that can't be answered this side of heaven. I could never be able to place a dollar amount on the damage that was done by a choice that I can never take back.

When the procedure was finished, I recall getting slowly off the procedure table, trying to ignore the pain and physical discomfort. I decided that I would pull myself up by my bootstraps, and deal with it. I decided I didn't need or want anyone to take care of me. I could do it myself, alone. After I finished getting dressed, I grabbed the papers and birth-control pills in the brown paper bag that the woman left on the desk for me. I was confident, or at least I decided I would act confident. I imagined that everything was going to be just fine as I pulled open the heavy door to leave the procedure room. I was so wrong!

I met the father in the waiting room and we walked silently out of the building. I left that place a changed woman. I had walked into that facility as a naive young girl who reluctantly handed the desk attendant my driver's license at the check-in window, and I left a broken woman who began to learn how to act "normal", walking out the door with my chin up, shoulders back, and determined to never think about "it" again. And so it began, the long dark season in my life that I was certain would never end.

My abortion was a secret that I worked very hard to keep buried; convinced that I would go to my grave never having told a soul. I didn't understand God's grace. I only figured He was waiting to severely punish me. I could not believe that His love and forgiveness was for someone like me – a murderer.

BUT GOD LOVED, FORGAVE AND HAD MERCY ON ME! And to that I now say, "THANK GOD!"

After 13 years of silence and heartache, I finally surrendered to God. He intervened and changed my life. The chains of shame, fear and silence that were so tightly bound around me, keeping me from what the Lord had called me to do, were all finally released. But they did not come off when I first met the Lord. Although I surrendered my life to Christ in 1995, I continued to carry the chains from my abortion until 2007. It was then that I truly faced that "lie" full-on and repented and surrendered ALL of me to The One Who Saves, my Redeemer Jesus Christ.

I have since answered His call into ministry as a Pastor and Counselor, and now lead a post-abortive healing ministry! Now that I have been set free and healed, I want others who have been impacted by abortion to know and experience how rich in mercy God truly is. Because of healing, I have been set free from all the chains that came with my abortion.

I write this with deep gratitude toward God for how He has reconciled me to himself through Jesus Christ. And I write this in honor of my daughter, Samantha Joy, the child I never held in my arms but will forever hold in my heart until we meet again in Paradise!

I love you Samantha, your life changed mine!
Pastor Paula Ellefson

Baby Facts

Angela Johnson from ProLife Across America asks: "Children – do we really look at them as a 'gift from God' or as a problem to avoid? Why is a new, precious gift of life not seen as one? Not only is it not celebrated, it's clearly not supported, culturally accepted or welcomed! Why is it seen as an inconvenience instead of a blessing from God?"[1]

Chapter 2
God Loves You

Genesis 1 speaks the beginning of everything to us: *"In the beginning God created the heavens and the earth. The earth was without form, and void; and darkness was on the face of the deep. And the Spirit of God was hovering over the face of the waters."* He alone created everything and then when He finished speaking it into existence, Genesis 2:7 says, *"... the LORD God formed man of the dust of the ground, and breathed into his nostrils the breath of life; and man became a living being."* So, He *spoke* all things into creation, but He *formed* and *breathed* life into mankind. We are fashioned in His likeness. Genesis 1:27 *"So God created man in His* own *image; in the image of God He created him; male and female He created them."* We, as human beings, are only a small part of what He has created and sustains.

When I have a few moments to think on these things, I find it challenging and nearly impossible to fathom how His conception of mankind was in His mind and that He wanted a relationship with us, so He established all of these things. John 1:1-5 tells us that *"In the beginning was the Word, and the Word was with God, and the Word was God. He was in the beginning with God. All things came into being through Him, and apart from Him nothing came into being that has come into being. In Him was life, and the life was the Light of men. The Light shines in the darkness, and the darkness did not comprehend it."* And we (mankind) became a living being to be the recipients of such a relationship and to be His light in the darkness of this world!

God sees all sin the same. He doesn't differentiate. To Him, sin is sin, that mankind needs to be witnessed to and delivered from. If we stand before Him and confess, repent and seek forgiveness, He will deliver us!

John 8:34 tells us that Jesus answered them saying, "Most assuredly, I say to you, whoever commits sin is a slave of sin. And a slave does not abide in the house forever, *but* a son abides forever. Therefore if the Son makes you free, you shall be free indeed.'"

To those who are born-again believers in Christ Jesus, God is our friend and companion, our creator, our originator, our deliverer, and our liberator; He is our everything!

Stop and actually envision the God of everything! Reflect in a focused manner on Him alone. How overwhelming is such contemplation! Such pondering generates boundless belief! How glorious He is!

Imagine if you can … how He spoke … and it was! He spoke a word of existence to something and it happened! What was nothing … is now … it exists! He created everything! ... *But,* He breathed His breath into mankind that we would be in a relationship with Him, we would communicate, we would walk together.

He had this plan from the very beginning. And to restore the relationship and make it everlasting, He sent His Son. He loved us first and still does! Love the Lord Your God with all of your heart, mind, will, and strength.

Abortion Fact

The Merriam-Webster dictionary offers this definition of abortion: "A medical procedure used to end a pregnancy and cause the death of the fetus. The termination of a pregnancy after, accompanied by, resulting in, or closely followed by death of the embryo or fetus: as a: spontaneous expulsion of a human fetus during the first 12 weeks of gestation (compare miscarriage) b: induced expulsion of a human fetus". [2]

Baby Facts

ProLife Across America informs us that from 1 day to 7 weeks, a new individual receives 23 chromosomes from each parent. He or she is truly a unique individual human being, never to be repeated. A new person has been created, who at this stage is a tiny living organism weighing only 15 ten-millionths of a gram. Life begins. On the first day of new life: the first cell divides into two, the two into four, and so on. Each of these new cells divides again and again as they travel toward the womb in search of a protected place to grow. At 18 days from conception, a baby's heart begins to beat, with its own blood.[1]

Believe it or not, 28 days from conception a baby has eyes, ears, and even a tongue! Muscles are developing along the future spine, and arms and legs are budding. In 30 days, the child has grown 10,000 times to 6 to 7mm (1/4 inch) long. Its brain has human proportions, and its blood flows in its veins. By 42 days, the skeleton is formed. The brain coordinates movement of muscles and organs and reflex responses have begun. Also by 42 days, the brain waves can be detected; the jaw forms, including teeth and taste buds. The unborn baby begins to swallow amniotic fluid. Its fingers and toes are developing.[1]

Forty-five days from conception, the unborn baby is making body movements, a full 12 weeks before the mother may notice such stirrings. By 7 weeks the chest and abdomen are fully formed. Swimming with a natural swimmer's stroke in the amniotic fluid, the baby now looks like a miniature human infant. Around 44 to 45 days, buds of milk teeth appear, and the unborn baby's facial muscles develop. Eyelids begin to form, protecting the developing eyes. Elbows take shape. Internal organs are present, but immature. 99% of muscles are present; each with its own nerve supply.[1]

At 52 days, spontaneous movement begins. The unborn baby then develops a whole collection of moves over the next 4 weeks including hiccupping, frowning, squinting, furrowing the brow, pursing the lips, moving individual arms and legs, head turning, touching his/her face, breathing (without air), stretching, opening the mouth, yawning and sucking.[1]

That by 8 weeks all organs function. And at 9 weeks the baby has individual fingerprints. Then at 10 weeks a baby can feel pain. Furthermore, by 12 weeks a baby can smile. Education is critical; in fact 94% of women regret their decision to abort according to ProLife Across America.[1]

Chapter 3
Preoccupied

At The Jonathan House, one ministry session was with a young woman, Elizabeth, who had extreme bitterness, unforgiveness, shame and guilt toward herself and her mother.

While her parents were married, her mother had numerous affairs with other men, and she divulged these wrong-doings to Elizabeth who loved her dad greatly, but admitted that he would sometimes go to the bar, stay too long and then come home drunk. Of course, this made her mother quite unhappy.

Her mother explained to Elizabeth that everything in her infidelity with the various men was alright and acceptable in society. (They regarded themselves as a "Christian" family because they took their children to church every Sunday, but certainly they were not living godly principles in front of their daughter.)

In her very late teens, Elizabeth told her mother that she was pregnant and asked her for advice. Her mother told her quite sternly that she should immediately get an abortion! Elizabeth was shocked! Nonetheless, she followed through with what her mother told her to do.

As time passed, Elizabeth became filled with hate, anger, unforgiveness and bitterness toward her mother for her insistence that she get an abortion. Elizabeth developed many extraordinary physical problems which came from not dealing with the underlying issues that she had stuffed down in her heart.

During her deliverance session, Elizabeth shared with us that she had phoned her pastor and told him what she had done, hoping to get godly counsel and help. He simply said, "You know that was wrong." And he hung up the phone. It was as if everyone in her life was preoccupied with their life and didn't really care about her. Thankfully, by the end of her deliverance session, Elizabeth was able to forgive and release her mother, the pastor, herself and others of the hurtful experiences.

Deuteronomy 30:19 says, "I call heaven and earth to witness against you today, that I have set before you life and death, blessing and curse. Therefore choose life, that you and your offspring may live,"

God gives us free will to choose and His word directs us to choose life. What do you choose?

Regardless whether a man or woman, the issue of abortion is devastating to a person because it carries so many sins, heartaches, and wrong thinking that it seems impossible to describe the feelings that so many people tell us they have.

At The Jonathan House, on the pre-ministry questionnaire, we ask, "Have you ever had an abortion, and if so, how many?" During their session they are instructed to confess and repent of their sin, and to forgive themselves and others. Evil spirits associated with the issue are then commanded to leave in the name of Jesus. This is a very intense time, even for men who requested or allowed the abortion procedure to happen.

As a part of the deliverance process, we have a life-like baby doll dressed in a sweet, warm outfit and placed in a matching soft blanket, that we hand to the person and ask them to hold it for a few minutes. We encourage them to snuggle it, name it, and talk to it as though it was their baby. When they have finished this quiet time, we counsel them to lay "their baby" at the foot of the cross, at the feet of Jesus. This moves deeply in their spirit, touching their hearts with the love of God. It creates an incredible healing in them. Confessing, repenting and forgiving produces absolute restoration!

Abortion Facts

The United States Supreme Court ruling of January 22, 1973, (Roe vs. Wade and Doe vs. Bolton) struck down the laws in all 50 states, allowing abortion – for any reason – up to the moment of live birth. The father of the child, even if he is married to the mother, has no legal right to prevent the abortion.[1]

Abortion is legal in America through all nine months of pregnancy. Over 1.3 million legal abortions occur in America each year. A sad irony: over two million couples wait to adopt – and that includes children of all races and those with special needs.[1]

Baby Facts

*Any Textbook Will Confirm What Every Doctor Knows
LIFE BEGINS AT CONCEPTION*[1]

*According to ProLife Across America by 8 weeks, it is now
a small-scale baby, at approximately 3 cm (1-1/8 inches)
and weighing a gram (1/30th of an ounce), yet well
proportioned. Every organ is present. The baby's heartbeat
is steady and its stomach produces digestive juices. Its liver
makes blood cells and the kidneys begin to function. Taste
buds are forming. Around 8-1/2 weeks, the unborn baby's
fingerprints are being engraved. Eyelids and palms of
hands are sensitive to touch. Also about 8 to 8-1/2 weeks,
of the 4500 structures in the adult body, 4000 are now
present in the unborn baby. The skeleton of the arms and
legs and the spine begins to stiffen as bone cells are added.
Then at 9 weeks from conception, the unborn baby will
bend fingers around an object placed in his/her palm,
unique fingerprints appear, and thumb sucking may occur.*[1]

*At 10 weeks, the unborn baby's body is sensitive to touch.
He/she squints, swallows, puckers up brow and frowns.
Eyelids, fingerprints and even fingernails are evident. Not
later than 11 weeks, the unborn now "practices" breathing,
since he/she will have to breathe air immediately after
birth. The baby urinates, and stomach muscles can now
contract. Vocal chords and taste buds form. Facial
expressions and even smiles are evident.*[1]

To Keep or Not To Keep

Chapter 4
She Couldn't Abort Me!

Although it happened many years ago I still remember the event as if it occurred yesterday. I was a sophomore in college, it was early afternoon, and I had just returned to my apartment after morning classes. Several of my roommates had also come back from class and were relaxing in the living room area when the phone rang. I picked up the receiver and heard the voice of the social worker I had been communicating with over the course of six months.

After a brief greeting, she announced that she had just been in contact with my biological mother. That statement knocked me off balance, but it was the next part that left me utterly stunned.

She told me that not only was my birth mom interested in meeting me, but so were the older brother and sister I never knew I had!

Though difficult to concentrate after those words, we discussed a few more details and closed the conversation by talking about the next steps and how to initiate contact with my family.

After I hung up the phone, I felt a combination of shock and devastation. I walked to my room, closed the door, collapsed on the floor, and began to sob uncontrollably for more than an hour. I didn't understand where all the pain or depth of emotion was coming from.

My mind also was filled with questions: Why did she give me up? Why had she kept my siblings and not me? The confusion and pain of rejection was so intense.

The family I had grown up with was always open with me about my adoption. In fact, I don't ever recall a time that I did not know I was adopted. It was a good home and I was the youngest of four – the other three being natural children of my adoptive parents.

As a young boy, I recall having daydreams about what my birth parents must have been like. I pictured in my mind images of them being beautiful, young, wealthy and perfect.

I often reasoned they must have given me up because of some difficult, but understandable circumstances. For example, perhaps they were too busy traveling the world to take care of a child.

On the other hand, buried in my imagination, I was sure they would want to find me someday and then any wrongs would be made right.

When that day would arrive they would then explain everything, all would be forgiven and we would be reunited and happy.

In that context, the desire to find them had always been with me and I looked forward to the day when I would be of legal age to begin the search. Following my 19th birthday, I began that process as soon as it was possible.

After the phone call with the social worker, I was filled with anticipation, but I was also very nervous. My birth mother and I started by writing letters to each other, first liaising through the department of social services, then eventually corresponding directly with each other.

Finally the day came when we had our first phone conversation. I can only describe that moment as surreal. We spoke for a long time. It felt foreign and awkward and at the same time it felt completely familiar and comfortable.

We were both amazed at how many things we had in common, including likes, dislikes, mannerisms and temperaments.

From the photos we had shared through the mail, we also both remarked how much we looked alike. We talked about little things and she also answered a few of the bigger questions I had for her.

She lived far away, but immediately invited me to visit her, and my brother and sister, in person offering to send me a plane ticket. Several months later I made the trip.

In those days non-passengers were allowed to walk to the gates at airports. My mother, sister and my sister's family came to meet me and were waiting at a designated place in the terminal. When I got off the plane, I walked toward the arranged location, spotted them first and stopped to watch them for a few moments.

I was practically paralyzed. They were looking around but didn't see me, so I eventually moved a bit closer. I came within a few feet, but then found myself unable to move any further.

I dropped my bag and once again began to weep. They then saw and ran over to me. We all hugged each other and cried together for a long time in the midst of a sea of people.

I spent roughly a week with my biological family during that visit. In that time I learned a lot about my mother and her life experiences. Very different from the grand scenarios I had created in my mind when I was growing up; I soon learned that my mother had had a troubled and complicated past.

She had been raised as the sole child in her home. Her conception came as a surprise to her parents as they were older in age. Her mother especially did not welcome the pregnancy and seemed to remain distant and harbor resentment toward my birth mom throughout their relationship. Growing up my mom had felt unloved and unwanted. She did however grow closer to her father over the years.

As time went on my mother found herself surrounded by unhealthy influences and people; the pain of rejection that she felt later manifested through rebellion. At a young age, she agreed to a marriage that she used primarily as a means of escape from the cold home environment.

Divorce however, followed after the birth of my brother and sister, as well as more years of running. After numerous harmful decisions and relationships, she was introduced to a man through a mutual friend. By that time she was so wounded that she had become very distrustful of men.

She warily decided to try again however, thinking that this new person might be worth meeting based on the encouragement and recommendation of her friend. While starting out well, things tragically changed.

On their first date my mother was raped and the man was never heard from again. That incident was the manner of my conception.

After that last disastrous experience, my mother became hateful of men. In addition to being bitter toward my biological father for the assault, she also resented the human (me) growing inside her. As far as she could see, the only solution was to terminate the pregnancy.

Since abortion was illegal in those days, she had to go "underground" and after some exploration found someone who would perform the procedure. The nurse, a woman, whom she was put in contact with, was reputed to be fail-proof when it came to carrying out abortions. The nurse and my mother arranged a time, agreed on a place, and then went ahead with the procedure.

Something unexpected occurred however. For some inexplicable reason, the abortion failed. A second attempt was made.

As my mother lay on the table and the operation was about to begin, something produced in her a sudden urge to stop. She mentioned she was going to leave, which the nurse simply didn't understand. The nurse tried to convince her to carry through with the abortion, but by then my mother was certain that God wanted her child to live.

Months later, I was born.

My mother had brought the pregnancy full-term despite the abortion attempts and several other physical traumas, including car accidents, a fall down a flight of stairs, and being kicked by a horse.

On the day she gave birth, she had been sleeping and dreamt that she was wetting the bed. Once she awoke, she realized that she was severely hemorrhaging. A friend phoned for an ambulance and she was taken to the emergency room. The doctors later told my mother that there were literally only minutes to spare to save both of our lives.

After giving birth to me, my mother went through a brief period of crisis. She was in conflict as to whether or not to give me up for adoption. The decision became even more difficult as her other children tried to convince her to keep their younger brother.

She eventually made up her mind and put me up for adoption, the only stipulation being was that she wanted me placed in a Christian home. Later when I met my birth mother, she gave me photos of that day. I still have with me pictures of her and my siblings holding me immediately before I was placed in temporary foster care.

More than ever, I am grateful and appreciative for my adoptive family having brought me into their home. I also realize how different my life could have turned out without them. Yet despite being raised in a good environment, I recall growing up plagued by feelings of rejection, anger and a chronic sense of sadness.

Similar to my biological mother, I acted out in unhealthy, rebellious ways, especially in my late high school and early adult years.

My manner of rebellion however usually manifested in subtle ways including withdrawal, rejection of myself and others, and self-destructive attitudes. I also experimented with drugs and alcohol, inappropriate relations with girls, and riding my motorcycle way too fast. Most of all, I found myself drawn to and pulled deeper and deeper into very dark music that ranged from being gloomy and violent to blatantly satanic.

Looking back I am amazed at the grip the music had on me because on one hand it produced a great sense of hopelessness, yet on the other hand felt thrilling and empowering. It was a vehicle through which I could express my anger, but at the same time, it contributed to making everything worse.

It became a terrible, downward spiral. There was something about the music that tapped into the core of my being. Something I couldn't quite define or put my finger on. Perhaps it may seem strange to some, but it was feeding something spiritual in me.

From a very young age I had been very interested in, and sensitive to, spiritual issues. During church and Sunday school, my mind would be filled with sensational imagery of God and epic battles between good and evil in the spiritual realms.

Ironically, at the same time I could easily become terrified by supernatural stories, movies or accounts of a demonic or occult nature. If I encountered something like that, I would find it difficult to sleep for weeks at a time.

This strange dynamic of fascination and fear of the spiritual remained with me into adulthood. Later I discovered and understood how God would use all of these life experiences, interests and personality characteristics to step into the call He had placed upon my life.

After college, I had practically abandoned my Christian faith. Whatever thread that remained was severed after my wife and I married and moved overseas. We went to Asia to teach, where we were exposed to people of very diverse cultural and religious backgrounds. Not having my feet firmly planted, they were quickly swept out from underneath me. My wife's faith however, grew stronger from our experience abroad.

Upon returning to the United States, we both started sensing a strong pull to go back to church. While new to us at the time, we would later understand that it had been the prompting of the Holy Spirit. God then began to apply the heat and bring me through a season of miraculous transformation.

It was as wonderful as it was difficult. At times it was extremely painful as I began to come to terms with some of my sin and poor life choices over the years.

God was not being cruel or mean to me. On the contrary, step by step He was bringing me to a place of healing and wholeness. As my wife and I grew in our faith, we began to get more exposure to the gifts of the Holy Spirit.

My excitement and fervor for the Lord began to soar and my deep desire and interest for spiritual things was revitalized, this time in a positive way. I started to learn more about healing ministries and one day heard that our church was hosting a one-day conference focused on healing through deliverance. I absolutely had to attend.

Toward the end of the conference, the speaker made a time of corporate prayer available asking everyone to stand and repeat after him as he led us through a prayer of release from generational bondage.

After praying, I found myself on my knees on the floor and my eyes were blinded. I then heard the kind and compassionate voices of the prayer ministers who had gathered around me. They gently asked me what I was experiencing.

I was confused and did not fully understand what was happening to me. I responded by saying that I had just gone through the prayer, but sensed there was some additional generational issues that God wanted to deal with.

I briefly told them about my biological mother. They asked if I had forgiven her, to which I replied "Yes."

Then they asked me if I had forgiven my biological father. I replied "No, I hadn't even thought of it." After they led me through another prayer, I then felt something leave me along with the blindness.

Although I didn't see them initially, later I met two of the several ministers who had been praying with me who were part of The Jonathan House Ministries. They encouraged me to visit with them for a more extensive ministry session.

God began to prepare me for that experience. I began to read as much material as I could find on the subject of healing and deliverance.

Over the next several months and through a series of promptings by the Holy Spirit, I knew when it was time and made the phone call to set up an appointment.

That meeting changed my life and altered my destiny. It is impossible to describe what the experience was like. So many things occurred. God began to liberate me from things like shame and heaviness that I had been carrying over my lifetime.

God also began to show me many pictures about my life, both before and after I was born. He even showed me battles that occurred in the spiritual realms.

Perhaps the most profound experience was that He revealed many things about my biological parents. I was utterly astonished by the level of spiritual oppression as we prayed about my father. It seemed that he had deep roots in the occult. As for my mother, it was almost unbelievable the effects that her choices, including the abortion attempts, had on me.

Strongholds of rejection and even death itself were torn down. I left the time of ministry with a sense of deep awe of God as well as gratitude for the gift of deliverance that He makes available for His kids. I understand His love for me at a level I never before could have imagined, and the heavy weight I had been carrying was lifted.

Something else I learned is that our spiritual adversary is very real and truly does desire to kill, steal and destroy in every way – physically, mentally, and spiritually. He attempts to exploit any opportunity available to him in order to harm and deceive us about God's truth, about God's healing and about God's salvation found in no other person than Jesus Christ.

I realize now that if he can't cause our physical death, he will attempt to cause abortion of the identity and destiny God has for our lives. Through my ministry experience, God affirmed His purposes for my life.

Today, I too, am involved with healing and deliverance ministry. I do this out of honor, respect, and response to God, but also out of simple gratitude. It is a deep joy for me to bless and give back to others, based on the immeasurable amount I have received.

To fellow survivors of abortion attempts, I want to let you know that God's healing is available to you. What the enemy intends for evil, the Lord can truly use for good and His glory.

To those parents who have attempted to abort their child, successfully or unsuccessfully, I wish to let you know that God's forgiveness and restoration is also available to you!

Know that there is nothing you could ever do that would remove His love or pursuit of you. Come and receive healing from the life-giver.

Finally, I wish to close by saying that today my biological family and me are doing well. I have seen them on occasion over the years and we remain in fairly regular contact. I can truly say that God has not only done a great work in me, but has done amazing things in them as well. They love Jesus, and God has not only brought them healing, but closeness to both Him and each other. God is good.

To Him be the glory!

Kurt K.

Baby Facts

Luke 1:44 reminds us, "For indeed, as soon as the voice of your greeting sounded in my ears, the babe leaped in my womb for joy."

At 12 weeks, though too small to be felt by the mother, the baby reaches peak frequency of movement during the third month. The baby's sex can be visually determined, and the child's eyes, ears and face begin to display distinctive characteristics. He/she can kick, turn feet, curl and fan toes, make a fist, move thumbs, bend wrists, turn head, open mouth and press lips tightly together. Now at 12 weeks, the unborn baby is about 3 inches long, weighing approximately 2 ounces. Fine hair begins to grow on his/her upper lip, chin and eyebrows. The baby swallows and responds to skin stimulations. [1]

And by 13 weeks, the unborn baby is yet about 3 inches long, weighing approximately 3 ounces. His/her facial expressions may resemble the parents. The baby is active, but baby is too small for mother to feel anything. Fourteen weeks from conception, the heart pumps several quarts of blood through the body every day. The unborn baby's eyebrows have formed and eye movement can be detected. At 15 weeks, in the growth development of the unborn baby, a wild production of nerve cells begins and continues for a month. A second surge will occur at 25 weeks. By now the baby also has an adult's tastebuds. [1]

Near 4 months, the unborn baby is now only 5-1/2 inches long, weighing approximately 5 ounces. He/she is actively moving about inside the safety of the womb. The baby turns, kicks and even somersaults – some of which can now be felt by the mother. Also at 4 months, bone marrow is now beginning to form and the unborn baby's heart is pumping 25 quarts of blood a day, reveals ProLife Across America. [1]

To Keep or Not To Keep

Chapter 5
I Chose Adoption

Another family had a teenage daughter, Harper, who made some inappropriate choices, left home for a short season, and ended up getting pregnant.

After discovering her pregnancy, she returned home.

Her mother, Abigail, was furious with her and became very bitter toward her.

Abigail decided she wanted to keep the baby or have her sisters keep it and raise it, but Harper did not accept that idea. She believed that her mother's anger and bitterness would be detrimental to the baby.

When the step-grandparents were told about the circumstances, they decided to counsel with Harper to see if they could persuade her to give birth to the child and arrange for the baby to be adopted. Harper was very much in favor of doing this and had a good pregnancy.

While pregnant, Harper decided she wanted a very precious Christian couple who attended her church to have her baby. The couple had been married several years and tried many times to have a child, but they were not able to conceive.

Harper approached the couple with the offer. They were elated and eagerly accepted! They agreed to pay all of her doctor and hospital expenses, and attorney fees for the arrangement.

What a blessing for that Christian couple as well as for Harper. Even though she had made a sinful choice earlier in her life, she now chose life for her baby.

Although you can see how Satan tried so many ways to prevent the adoption from happening, I know that our Lord was working in this situation, because in spite of the sin early in her life, God was glorified by her choice of letting the child be adopted by the Christian couple.

What a miracle!

1 John 1:9 says, *"If we confess our sins, He is faithful and just to forgive us our sins and to cleanse us from all unrighteousness."*

Baby Facts

ProLife Across America goes on to say that at 4-1/2 months from conception, the baby is still very small (less than 8 inches in length), but it can have dream (REM) sleep. Nostrils and toenails become visible. Also at 4-1/2 months, the unborn baby's ears are functioning by the end of the 4th month and he/she hears the mother's heartbeat, as well as external noises like music. The baby is also able to experience pain. Life-saving surgery has been successfully performed on babies at this age. From 18 to 20 weeks, the baby has grown in size approximately 7-1/2 inches long and 14 ounces in weight. His/her movements can now be felt by the mother, including the baby's hiccups.[1]

To Keep or Not To Keep

Chapter 6
Release Them

There was a family whose youngest son, Lucas, was walking with the Lord. He had accepted Jesus while he was in a Christian grade school camp. In his teen years Lucas, like most of the other young boys, dated a pretty girl and then went too far in the relationship. He did not know that Ginger got pregnant and had an abortion on her own without telling him.

However, some months later, Ginger divulged it to him. Lucas was very upset and shared this news with his sister, Maggie – not his parents!

Years after that, he married a woman, Jane, who had two children from a previous marriage and they were then blessed with two children of their own.

When Lucas and Jane were very young, they lived close to Lucas' parents in a rural area and his parents were in the process of remodeling a beautiful old house. While working on the project, Lucas' mother found a nest of baby mice in one of her cupboards. Since her husband was not home at the time, she phoned Lucas and asked him to quickly come up to their home and kill this nest of baby mice. When he arrived he informed his mom and said, "Mom, I can't kill those baby mice. I'll take them out back to the field behind the barn in the woods and release them so they can live!'"

His mother never forgot that sweet moment when Lucas spoke those words.

That life-filled statement made a lasting impression in her heart! She knew Lucas would never have had his baby aborted!

Matthew 5:21 "You have heard that it was said to those of old, 'You shall not murder, and whoever murders will be in danger of the judgment.'"

Abortion Facts

Abortionists lie in this manner: They know part of dehumanizing an unborn child includes lying to the mothers about what the child really is. Moms always want to know the sex, but they lie and say, "It's too early to tell." It's better for the women to think of the fetus as an "*it*." Mothers-to-be are never allowed to look at the ultrasound because abortionists know that if they so much as heard the heartbeat, the mothers wouldn't want the abortion. Abortionists know that once a mother sees an ultrasound photo, she can clearly see her unborn baby is a person, not an "*it*." Abortion is not a game. It ALWAYS ends in the death of a child. Studies show that between 70 to 90% of women who see a sonogram of their unborn baby choose life and reject abortion. Sonograms show an incredibly powerful image and can mean instant *conversion*. Women can be saved from a lifetime of guilt for having been swayed to abort their child.

Baby Facts

At 5 months, each side of the baby's brain now has a billion nerve cells. If a sound is especially loud, the unborn baby may jump in reaction to it. Thumb-sucking has been observed during the 5th month. Also during 5 to 6 months, the unborn baby practices breathing by inhaling amniotic fluid into its developing lungs. The baby will increase seven times in weight and nearly double in height. At 6 months from conception, fine hair grows on eyebrows and head. Eyelash fringe appears. The unborn baby's weight is about 640 grams (22 ounces), height 23 cm (9 inches). Babies born at this age have survived, according to ProLife Across America.[1]

Chapter 7
How Can This Be?

Abortions happen in Christian families as well. Here is a story of parents who found out about their children's choices after the abortion procedures had occurred.

Although being a Christian family, Isaac and Sara had children who each made some very regretful choices. Their oldest son, Eric, in the later years of high school dated Madison, a very sweet, but emotionally hurting girl. Her parents divorced when she was young, and she was living with her father. Her birth mom lived in another state. Eric's family welcomed her into their family and treated her with love and acceptance and became very close to her through those dating years. Everything appeared to be proceeding properly.

Then a receipt for $500.00 accidently dropped out of Eric's pocket onto the floor, and his parents found it. They couldn't imagine what that receipt was for! So, after much prayer and investigation, they discovered that Eric borrowed $500.00 from a friend of theirs to pay for an abortion for Madison. The family was greatly disappointed and extremely saddened to learn about the situation, but continued to love and accept the two of them.

After a short time, Eric and Madison's relationship deteriorated and the two of them went their separate ways. Regrettably, due to ignorance of the parents in this area, the abortion issue was not properly addressed within the family. It was very perplexing for this Christian family to accept the fact that their son had paid to have his baby destroyed before it was born.

Eric later accepted the Lord Jesus as his Savior and ended up marrying, Ava, a Christian woman and they had two lovely daughters. The entire family is now walking in the path of our Lord Jesus and serving Him.

Another incident that we dealt with affecting that family was with their teen-aged daughter, Sue. Sue had accepted the Lord early in grade school. Once a week after school she led a class, teaching her friends about Jesus. She revealed Him in every area of her life and while she was in upper grade school was even responsible for her parents accepting Jesus as their Lord and Savior. Isaac and Sara were very proud of her and they trusted her completely.

When Sue was in her late teens, she asked if she could spend the summer with her Christian grandparents who lived in another state. Her parents granted her request and blessed her as they sent her off on a new adventure at her grandparent's home. It was a great summer. Sue obtained a job as a cashier at a local restaurant.

Later in the season, unbeknownst to Isaac and Sara, a boyfriend, Ian, from her home state contacted her and they met in another town and ended up having sex. Sue became pregnant, and they resolved to get an abortion before the summer was over. Neither her grandparents nor her parents knew anything about this situation.

Sue returned home at the end of the summer and began her junior year in high school. At the end of high school, she went to work and met a nice young man, Tyler. They dated for a year or so, and that relationship led to marriage.

After marriage, Sue and Tyler had two sons, just 18 months apart, and all was going well. Their entire family attended church and they were raising their sons in a very godly home, teaching them to love the Lord as well as the importance to pray each day. Their oldest son accepted Jesus as his Lord and Savior in the early years of grade school.

After a few years passed, the younger son developed some very serious health issues and was very ill for several years. He required substantial care, many doctor visits, and a great amount of home care – which Sue and Tyler were able to do quite well. After a few years, the Lord miraculously healed the younger son from his severe health issues. It was such a blessing to the whole family! And when he was about 7 years old, he too accepted Jesus into his heart.

At this time, however, Sue went to her parents and confessed the sin that she had committed when she was a young teenager. She admitted what happened during that summer she spent in another state with her grandparents when Ian visited her, how they secretly met in another town, had sex and then discovered she was pregnant. She went on explaining how she and Ian decided that she needed to have an abortion. Isaac and Sara were extremely shocked to hear that news, especially since Sue was such a great Christian young woman. They forgave her and life went forward for them all. The issue was never mentioned again.

However, as the years went forward, Sue and Tyler divorced, and a couple of years later she married another Christian man, Aiden, and everything appeared to be normal. In the meantime, Isaac and Sara, her parents, moved to another state to be near their aging parents.

Sue was still quite young and had been in excellent health all of her life when suddenly she began experiencing health concerns over the next several years. The doctors had difficulty trying to find the cause of the illnesses. Subsequently, Sue shared her abortion issue with her physician. Finally, one of her doctors suggested she see a Christian counselor where Sue received weekly counseling for several months and obtained emotional freedom from the sin of aborting her baby.

While we are free to make our own decisions, we must understand what that truly means. Matthew 16:19 says, "And I will give you the keys of the kingdom of heaven, and whatever you bind on earth will be bound in heaven, and whatever you loose on earth will be loosed in heaven." If we "loose" our poor choice; then we'll reap the consequences of that poor choice.

Proverbs 18:21 says, *"Death and life are in the power of the tongue."* If our choice is abortion, and we speak that out, we are declaring death. If we carry through with the decision, our spirit knows we have committed murder. We need to go before God with witnesses and confess, repent, forgive and ask for forgiveness. Confessing, repenting, and forgiving are necessary for healing. Others will have influenced your decision, and you need to forgive them. Just as important – you need to forgive yourself. God, our Deliverer, will guide you through this process.

"It is important to appreciate that a person is a person from the very moment the sperm and the egg join together to form an embryonic human being. The arguments by the pro-abortionists about whether life begins at twelve weeks, fourteen weeks, twenty-eight weeks or birth are all built on the dictates of secular convenience as opposed to the reality of spiritual truth and understanding. In that minute of assemblage of living material is all that is needed to determine the sex, character, personality, body shape, and looks of the person, but more important than the flesh potential (soul and body characteristics), is the fact that the spirit of the child already resides there." [3]

"We have, for example, delivered people of a spirit of rejection that entered during the very act of sex that resulted in the embryonic child... Rejection is a particularly powerful and dangerous form of abuse... But a child who is the victim of rejection is vulnerable to being accepted and 'owned' by the demonic, causing much pain and anguish throughout life." All demonic areas are curable through deliverance, provided that the person is willing to forgive and he/she deals rightfully with any other basics that have not been resolved in his/her life. [3]

Genesis 4:7 says that "sin is crouching at your door." (NIV) One ancient rendering of this verse refers to a demon waiting to get in. Cain opened himself up to Satan's control and a spirit of murder entered. [3]

In ministry we have dealt with people who have been involved in murder – usually the murder related to willingly having an abortion. We then cast out a spirit of murder from the person who chose to have the abortion. If the person is truly repentant, they are delivered from a spirit of death. There must be repentance from the sin that gave the demon a right of entry and the blood of Jesus restores you. [3]

Chapter 8
The Great Deception

Certainly we all know that by the law of the land following Roe vs. Wade, a person has the *right* to choose to make abortion their *option*. What they don't comprehend and grasp is what making that decision does to our human spirit. How we will actually process that outcome is beyond our intellectual capacity. Man is robbing the very thing God desires. In John 10:10 Jesus articulates this to us, saying that: "The thief does not come **except** to steal, and to kill, and to destroy. I have come that they may have **life**, and that they may have *it* more **abundantly**." (Emphasis added.)

Yes, God says life – and have it *more* abundantly! The ability for us to choose to remove, murder, or destroy the precious gift of life He puts in a woman's body, is ours to make. So the world says. But that choice comes at a high price! Those making such a decision do not realize how high that price is. Not one person honestly communicates the ramifications to those making a nearly unbearable choice. There is no list of consequences spoken of during the decision making time. There are no real alternatives discussed. Repercussions are not important in the dialogue shared, and in fact, are nearly nonexistent.

But, it's "Your option to choose abortion." The verbiage goes something like this: "You won't have to explain it to your family and friends." (Here comes guilt.) "It's best not to have anyone know." (Here comes secrecy, deception, concealment, suppressing of feelings.) "It's not so bad." (Here comes the justification of murder.) "It's better than keeping the baby and feeling ashamed for getting pregnant in the first place." (Feelings of shame come for sure!)

And on and on the excuses are presented to you so you'll know just what to say should it be uncovered. Yes, you have a choice. But the depression, the despair, sadness, downheartedness, hopelessness, and gloominess that come are beyond your thinking! The misery of taking a life, the burying of joy and losing all hope is so undermining to the person making the decision. It is not a choice! It's a death sentence not only to the baby, but to the mother's spirit (and the father too, if he's in on the decision)! Such discouragement, demoralization, disheartening, and crushing comes upon you from the evil one that you don't think you'll see the light again. Along with the spirits of death and murder, other debilitating spirits come, some of which are previously listed, and so many, many, more.

Out goes self-respect and self-esteem, and in pours pride, secretiveness, guilt, shame, disgrace, humiliation, and dishonesty. All of these negative spirits affect all of our personal relationships – at work, at home, and at play. There they are – hidden, deep-rooted, and entrenched – waiting for the moment to raise their evil heads, grasping at our spirit and pulling us down even further. We cannot be the same until we expose the truth, ask for forgiveness, repent, forgive ourselves and come before God to experience His unconditional love. Having witnesses to this process is preferred. Matthew 18:16 references this: "that 'by the mouth of two or three witnesses every word may be established.'"

Did you know that generational sin goes back three generations, but sexual sins go back ten generations? We need to have these broken off of us and our families. God wants us to experience His freedom, His forgiveness, and His love. He does not want us to be held in bondage by the one who wants you to live in discouragement, dismay, dismay of mind and heart, mental anguish, mental torment, and every spirit under his control (Apollyon – the destroyer). The evil one wants rebellion and disobedience and the thief and lying spirit to live and flourish in you. He also wants the spirit of pride, haughtiness, contention, perfection, self-righteousness, all religious spirits, the spirit of failure, self-hate, death, death wish, premature death, and suicide to reign in you. He wishes for you to suffer from sexually transmitted diseases and the spirit of divorce. He intends to try to control you in all areas of your being.

In the Merriam-Webster Thesaurus, aborting is "terminating, ending, abandoning, canceling, halting, stopping, quitting, calling off, calling to a halt, stopping midstream, or breaking off." [2]

When it is life we're talking about, it matters to God who is the Creator of that life! And it matters to our spirit and to us. We are not counseled to know what this experience will be like nor what the effect or the consequence will be. To murder, to abandon life itself has drastic, shameful, immoral outcomes. God wants us to know that to offer life to a child is a blessing to that baby, to you, and to someone who desperately wants a child that they cannot conceive on their own. Even with adoption, you will have to come against the evil one and be restored by God, but not because of murder. You will still need to confess, repent and ask forgiveness for your sexual sin.

Galatians 5:16-21 says, *"I say then: Walk in the Spirit, and you shall not fulfill the lust of the flesh. For the flesh lusts against the Spirit, and the Spirit against the flesh; and these are contrary to one another, so that you do not do the things that you wish. But if you are led by the Spirit, you are not under the law. Now the works of the flesh are evident, which are: adultery, fornication, uncleanness, lewdness, idolatry, sorcery, hatred, contentions, jealousies, outbursts of wrath, selfish ambitions, dissensions, heresies, envy, murders, drunkenness, revelries, and the like; of which I tell you beforehand, just as I also told you in time past, that those who practice such things will not inherit the kingdom of God."*

God alone gives us the Spirit, as in Galatians 5:22-25 *"But the fruit of the Spirit is love, joy, peace, longsuffering, kindness, goodness, faithfulness, gentleness, self-control. Against such there is no law. And those who are Christ's have crucified the flesh with its passions and desires. If we live in the Spirit, let us also walk in the Spirit."* He longs for us to be filled with and carriers of Love, Joy, Peace, Patience, Kindness, Goodness, Faithfulness, Gentleness, and Self-control. With these in us permanently, we are His and He is ours.

To Keep or Not To Keep

Chapter 9
Living with Aftereffects

For the last three weeks in March of 2015, we here in Minnesota have had remarkably warm weather for this season. After being covered with ice and snow for several months, at a moment's notice the tulips and crocuses have come through the rich, black, soil in our backyard. They've come back to life and raised their beautiful stems to grow and blossom. The crocuses opened their beautiful flowered heads to say "hello" to spring. Unfortunately, the next day the Lord sent 10 inches of heavy, white snow to cover them – as well as all of the other greenery that thought it was time to come alive again. God always provides for their care, so I know they will come back in the proper time to bring forth His beautiful design!

Regrettably, our lives are comparable to that at times. Like those spring blooms which decide for themselves to drive through the dirt at the earliest possible moment, we make choices or have others in our family or friendship circle make choices that make us feel like we have 10 inches of heavy lead on our backs. Instead of snow like the flowers feel, we have an alternative heaviness that restrains us. God alone can heal those undesirable decisions we have made and subsequently develop our lives to bring glory and honor to Him.

Countless people of God make wrong, immoral, and poor choices when carrying these heavy loads, thus they unfortunately pay the price in diverse ways. I am saddened to say that both young and old alike make poor choices. Life is a precious jewel that we often take for granted and it becomes so easy for people to end a precious life without really thinking of the consequences of their decision. They pay a big price for that misguided conclusion and then live with the aftereffects for years.

Mike Huckabee wrote on Facebook, "Life begins at conception. This is not just a Biblical view — it is affirmed by modern science and every unique human DNA schedule, which is present at conception. Our value, and celebration, of every unique human life is the basic tenet of our freedom and should never be abandoned. I personally pray for the day when law matches the science and we support and honor every life from conception. I appreciate the efforts toward the Pain-Capable Unborn Child Protection Act." [4]

The Pain-Capable Unborn Child Protection Act:
- Amends the federal criminal code to prohibit any person from performing or attempting to perform an abortion except in conformity with this Act's requirements. [4]

- Requires the physician to first determine the probable post-fertilization age of the unborn child, or reasonably rely upon such a determination made by another physician, by making inquiries of the pregnant woman and performing such medical examinations and tests as a reasonably prudent physician would consider necessary.[4]

- Prohibits the abortion from being performed if the probable post-fertilization age of the unborn child is 20 weeks or greater, except: (1) where necessary to save the life of a pregnant woman whose life is endangered by a physical disorder, illness, or injury, excluding psychological or emotional conditions; or (2) where the pregnancy is the result of rape, or the result of incest against a minor, if the rape has been reported at any time prior to the abortion to an appropriate law enforcement agency, or if the incest has been reported at any time prior to the abortion to an appropriate law enforcement agency or to a government agency legally authorized to act on reports of child abuse or neglect. Permits a physician to terminate a pregnancy under such an exception only in the manner that provides the best opportunity for the unborn child to survive, unless that manner would pose a greater risk than other available methods would pose of the death or substantial and irreversible physical impairment of a major bodily function, excluding psychological or emotional conditions, of the pregnant woman.[4]

- Subjects individuals who violate this Act to a fine, imprisonment for not more than five years, or both. Bars prosecution of a woman upon whom an abortion is performed in violation of this Act for violating or conspiring to violate this Act.[4]
- Defines "abortion" to mean the use or prescription of any instrument, medicine, drug, or any other substance or device to intentionally kill an unborn child or to intentionally terminate a pregnancy with an intention other than: (1) after viability, to produce a live birth and preserve the life and health of the child; or (2) to remove a dead unborn child.[4]
- Would limit many abortions based on the child's ability to feel pain, but know that even this is but a step in the direction of hopefully one day protecting every life.[4]

Mike Huckabee continued, "As Governor, I promoted and signed a fetal protection act. I imposed a ban on partial birth abortion, established waiting periods, created parental notification requirements, and passed a bill so mothers who brought a newborn to a hospital or fire station would not be prosecuted for child abandonment. I will always stand for the sanctity of all human life from the moment of conception until the grave." [4]

Chapter 10
The Effects on Others

Being a moral and honorable Christian woman, Sophia set high standards and expectations for her grown children and grandchildren. As Sophia discovered that some of her children had abortions previous to being married, it really damaged her thinking and heart as she began to take responsibility in her mind and spirit for the things her children had done. She began to wonder if the abortions could have been prevented if she had raised them and taught them differently about all of these sinful things.

She had always been in excellent health, but when her husband was at work all day Sophia very often dwelt on undesirable thoughts, carrying the blame for her children's past actions. As she continued to concentrate day after day on the family issues, Sophia began to develop some very significant physical problems. Within one year, she developed a rare neurological issue, experienced problems with her thyroid, developed shingles; began to have problems with high blood pressure, problems with gout in both of her feet, and if that wasn't enough, she became very weak and almost fainted when she was carrying her groceries into the house. After seeing different doctors, Sophia was finally sent for expensive and time consuming treatment several times a week that went on for several months. Within the next year, the Lord healed each of those health issues.

They lived in a rural area and during Sophia's half hour of walking each morning, she talked to the Lord. She would walk along the country road and would pass a small country church that had a cemetery close by. During her prayer time, she primarily felt she should pray for her family. One day, she sensed the Lord telling her to go home and make a small wooden cross, get a shovel and return to the cemetery. Sophia thought and prayed about it for several days as she continued walking past the cemetery. Finally, after several weeks had passed, she decided to symbolically "bury" the past and do what had been on her heart for herself and the Lord.

But when the day came, as she was cleaning and doing the morning chores in the kitchen, she was listening to Christian radio – which was her habit. On James Dobson's radio program he was speaking about issues similar to what had happened in Sophia's life and in the lives of her family members. It was truly a God ordained program for that day in her life! At the close of the radio program, the Lord took away all of the guilt and shame that Sophia had allowed the enemy to put in her life dealing with the choices her children previously made! Freedom came forth in a mighty way! She did not have to go to the cemetery to "bury" those thoughts because they were truly given over to the Lord and freedom came into her life!

All of the diseases Sophia developed had come because of the abortion issues. Stuffing the root of abortion gave Satan a place to settle down in her life. Even though Sophia herself did not abort a baby, the guilt she felt about not being a "better" mother went deep into her spirit and greatly affected her health for a time. Once she dealt with the fear of failure, pain, guilt, and shame, God began His healing and eventually brought total restoration.

1 Peter 5:7 "Give all your worries and cares to God, for he cares about you."

Abortion Facts

Studies show there are an estimated 40 to 50 million abortions every year in the world! On average, that's 125,000 abortions each day!

On April 7, 2015, the Worldometers' counter for abortions worldwide for the year 2015 was at 11,112,057.[5]

By October 7, 2015 (six months later), the Worldometers' counter for abortions worldwide for the year 2015 had already risen to 32,230,718; having increased by over 21 million abortions in only six months.[5]

Baby Facts

ProLife Across America says that during 25 to 28 weeks from conception, the unborn baby can recognize his/her mother's voice. The baby is using four of the five senses (vision, hearing, taste, and touch), opens and closes his eyes, and knows the difference between waking and sleeping, and can relate to the moods of the mother. At 8 months, the unborn baby's skin becomes pink and smooth. The pupils of the eye respond to light. Also at 8 months, the unborn baby's weight increases by 1 kg. (over two pounds) and his/her living quarters inside the mother's womb are becoming cramped. Around 8 months, the unborn baby's fingernails reach to the tip of the finger. The skin begins to thicken, with a layer of fat stored underneath for insulation and nourishment. 8 months from conception, the unborn baby swallows a gallon of amniotic fluid each day and often hiccups. Though movement is limited, due to the cramped quarters the baby's kicks are stronger, and mother may be able to feel an elbow or heel against her abdomen.[1]

To Keep or Not To Keep

Chapter 11
While We Were Yet Sinners

My parents married in November of 1958 and I was born in October of 1959. My childhood and adolescent years were filled with memories of a hard-working father who was seldom at home, and yet when the latter half of the week and weekends came, he would drink heavily in the evenings when he was at home. My mother was an angry, domineering woman who returned to work outside the home when I was in junior high school. Even as a young child and throughout the years growing up, daily verbal and physical beatings were not uncommon, and trying to protect my two younger brothers from experiencing the "Wrath of Mom" as we referred to her behavior, was not an easy task. Looking back, I understand now why I was sexually active in my teen years, searching to be genuinely and sincerely loved, but my poor choices and the consequences of those decisions would go on to affect me and others for years thereafter.

I attended Catholic grade school until fifth grade, and then went on to public schools for the remainder of my education. I remember Roe vs. Wade in 1973, and how my parents were pleased that if someone would become pregnant, there was a legalized method to end an unwanted pregnancy. They would talk about girls or young women who would go off and have abortions illegally, and sometimes have complications or horrible bleeding, and about other young, pregnant women who left the area, had the baby, and came back later without the child.

As part of her verbal abuse, I remember in my high school years being told by my mother that she wished she had an abortion when she was pregnant with me: because my father had beat her one month after they married and she would have left him; because I was nothing but trouble all those years; that she was trapped because of me; and the list went on and on. Thinking back, I can only remember one time my father ever defended me against my mother and all he said was "Would you just leave the kid alone?"

My father always wanted "his boys" (his sons, his nephews) to go hunting and fishing with him, but as he put it "It was no place for a woman to be." Recently, at my father's twin brother's funeral, a few of my male cousins shared stories about my father and uncle taking them hunting, fishing and having taught them to drive. At least I can say that my father did teach me how to drive a vehicle.

I was a rebellious teen; basically because I felt unloved and was told repeatedly how I would never amount to anything. I pushed hard to complete my schooling so I could leave home. I graduated from high school three months after I turned 17 in January of 1977, and was working full-time shortly thereafter, paying room and board, and yet was still their housekeeper. Nothing was ever good enough or satisfying enough to please either of my parents. I finally had enough and moved out on my own in April of 1977. My first pregnancy occurred sometime in May and I crossed the stage at the high school graduation ceremony pregnant. I told my parents later in June that I was pregnant, but only after the baby's father had started repeatedly pinning me on the floor, slapping me in the face and torso, and tickling me to the point that I hurt or lost control of my bladder. I really was caught in between two abusive relationships with him and my parents.

I can remember telling my father that I was pregnant. His first question was "Do you love him?" and I said "No." He then said "You're getting an abortion. I'll be damned if I'm going to raise your kid." He took me in the house and told my mother to schedule an appointment, and that she was to take me to Chicago to have it done. She told me that she was appalled that I would make her a grandmother before she was 40 years old. I went back to my apartment alone and cried. In the days that followed, I went to several pregnancy help services confused as to what to do. But my parents were insistent and so on a bright, sunshiny day in July, my mother took me to an abortion clinic on Michigan Avenue in Chicago. It turned out to be the first of four abortions in my life.

I remember the cathedral-shaped windows, the poppy-orange, stackable, plastic chairs in the waiting room, the steam registers, and my mother's disdainful and sneering face. I remember being called in to have the procedure and the nurse telling my mother that she could not be in the procedure room; that she must wait in the waiting room. The nurse kept calling the baby a fetus as she went through the clinic's disclaimers and protocol, telling me how I'd get back to normal with my life after this was done and I could forget about everything and move on. What a lie! There were so many young women and teens in the clinic that day. There must have been 30 of us in the recovery room. Some were crying. Others had the attitude of "Hey, it's just another method of birth control. You'll be fine." On the ride home, I was silent. My mother broke the silence with "Do you want to talk?" I responded, "You want to talk now! You had this done two years ago and you want to talk now after you knew the pain. No! It's too late to talk." And I fell silent.

My parents stated that I needed to move back home until I turned 18 and I obeyed them. I should have left for another state of the union, but I went back to their home. It was an even greater hell on earth than ever before, so to cope I enrolled in the local junior college, took two classes and continued to work. I quit junior college after one semester, changed jobs and went to work full-time where I met my first husband in March of 1978 and moved out of my parents' home at that time. We married later that year and had difficulty becoming pregnant. I blamed myself because of the abortion and each month was saddened when my period would come anywhere from five to eight weeks apart. Eventually God blessed us with a daughter in 1981 and then with a son a year later.

I can remember my parents speaking to my toddler children with the same harsh tone of voice that they used with me, and it was then that I greatly limited any visits between my parents and children. I did not want the poison of their toxic mindsets to be instilled in my children. It is still beyond my comprehension how grandparents could push for the abortion of their first or any of their grandchildren. It reveals how the prince of this world has darkened the understanding and hardened the hearts of the unbelievers, as it says in Ephesians 4:18.

The marriage to my children's father lasted until 1985. He was striving to be a success in business, typically working 12 hour days, and our relationship waned. I was with the children while he was gone to work. He'd get in at 8:30 or 9:00 at night and the children would be asleep or crabby because they were ready for bed. The marriage ended for many reasons including my unhappiness, our quite opinionated mothers, our lack of communication, and the pain of my past.

My second, third, and fourth abortions were all about a year apart. In my promiscuity and numerous relationships I was seeking to find love and to be loved. In a strange way, my lifestyle was an attempt to heal from the hurt, but in actuality it was causing more hurt and pain both for me and the men that I had been involved with. My sexual relations seemed no different than a handshake. They were just physical needs to be met and if a pregnancy would occur, abortion was the final birth control method. I had been told by my parents that I could not handle raising more than two children, that two children were more than enough to handle financially, and to give the children the attention that they needed.

My last pregnancy was conceived in July of 1987, ironically ten years after the first abortion. The fellow was a casual friend and we had been intimate. Afterward, we were walking and talking about what I do not recall, but I had this unique sensation, a tingling in my uterus and I remember saying to him, "Oh my God, I just got pregnant!" He said "How do you know?" I said "I just felt it. Something's happened. It is so different." The sensation was different than any orgasm. It was not a cramp, and my body did not eliminate any fluids. I just knew that I had just conceived. Sure enough, three weeks later I still had not started my menstrual cycle and the pregnancy test result was positive.

By this time I felt like an old pro at having abortions. I called and scheduled the appointment, arranged for a girlfriend to watch my two children, and proceeded to drive myself to the clinic. But that day was different. I had a confidence about myself, and a certainty that no one, except for my friend watching my children, would know about the procedure. I got to the clinic, went through the disclosures and facility protocol, signed the papers, paid for the procedure, and waited. The whole occurrence was no different to me at that time than going to the dentist or the eye doctor. I was called to the room, got on the table, and my feet were placed in the stirrups. As they strapped my ankles and told me to lie down, I heard a resounding voice that thundered "Not one more of my children!" The voice was so loud it sounded like it went straight through my heart.

I said "Stop the procedure! Don't do it!" The nurse said "You're here. It's paid for. It'll be over with soon." I again said "No, don't do it." And I heard "Be still or you'll get ripped up." One of the nurses put her hand on my shoulder and held me still. I then saw the canister with white, fibrous, cotton, gauze material off to the left of me, go from white to fresh, red blood splattering and filling the container. The sound of the machine with the whirring and vacuuming suction that I had heard three times earlier in my life lasted for a minute or so, and then there was silence. My insides felt suctioned flat. My legs and hips trembled and it was difficult to walk. In my mind I knew that I had heard the voice of God. When I looked at the doctor and nurses, the expression on their faces looked pleased, like they completed another job well done.

I was released from the recovery room and had a long drive home alone to think about what happened before I had to pick up my two living children. My heart was ripped to shreds remembering the sound of that voice. My friend looked at me with the expression on her face of "How could you have done such a thing?" but she said, "I'm here for you if you need me." I could say nothing but, "I'm okay. I'll be okay." But I wasn't okay, and I wasn't going to be okay.

The memory of what occurred continued to torment me and a year later on October 8, 1988, I had an emotional or mental breakdown. I sought help for depression, but in effect only put a bandage on something that needed surgery.

Looking back, I can see how the pain that both of my parents experienced as children affected their lives, due to the environment they grew up in. My paternal grandfather left the family when my father and his twin brother were just 18 months old. My grandmother was left with eight children to raise and a dairy farm to manage, and yet she still held the family together through the Great Depression. My maternal grandparents experienced shattered dreams when my grandfather was diagnosed with ALS (Lou Gehrig's disease) shortly after my mother's birth. My grandmother became bitter as she was then forced to be the breadwinner of the family with an ailing husband versus having more children and a different lifestyle than what she experienced.

There were many years of pain that followed. I had remarried a man who turned out to be caught in addictions, and was physically and mentally abusive. During that time I was placed on prescription medications for about three years. I still have difficulty remembering my children's high school years because the pain had been so intense.

But God! Twelve years after the emotional breakdown, on August 24, 2000 at the age of 40, I received Jesus as my Lord and Savior. Not even a year later, my second husband announced to me, after he had been gone for three days (unknown as to where), that he wanted out of the marriage. The Bible says to let the unbeliever go if they so choose to go, and so I did. He remarried within three months to another woman and I have not seen him in over a decade and a half. As I said then and I say now, "Good luck, goodbye and good riddance!" I couldn't see too much good at that time, but deep inside, and through the counsel of godly brothers and sisters, I knew that God had a plan for my life.

I had endured most of the first forty years of my life in abusive relationships, either receiving abuse or being abusive. It is true that hurting people hurt others and I was guilty of that more than I would care to remember. I knew I was not worthy. The memory of the four abortions and the realization of those lost hopes and dreams for those children was a huge torment. Even after receiving Jesus

Christ as my Lord and Savior, Satan attempted to keep me in bondage and to keep me from seeking help, by saying things like "Some Christian you are, killing your own babies." "What are you going to say (or do) when these Christians find out about what you've done? What are you going to do then?" I learned that fear and things kept in darkness would allow the devil to gain a stronghold to keep me in bondage, so I sought out a Christian counselor who suggested that I check with the local crisis pregnancy center and inquire about receiving counseling there.

In February of 2003, I called the Crisis Pregnancy Center and spoke with the director about the Post Abortion Recovery Program. She was a loving woman who shared that it was a 14 week program and that it would be the hardest thing that I would ever do, but it would be the most rewarding thing that I would ever do. She made it clear that the devil is a liar and he has us believing his lies about us, about situations that happened to us, about what we have done, and about the forgiveness that is available through Jesus Christ in that it has already been paid for. But God is bigger than the devil and Jesus has already defeated him, and Jesus has already taken back the keys to death, hell and the grave, and we are more than a conqueror through Christ Jesus. She told me that if I would commit to this time of one-on-one counseling, she would go through it with me and we would witness what Jesus would do in the healing and restoration power through the blood of Jesus Christ.

Well, she was absolutely right that it was the hardest 14 weeks I had ever encountered in my life, but it was also the most rewarding. Freedom came in because there were no more lies, nothing was hidden, because of forgiveness toward my parents and toward the men that were involved in my past, and because I forgave myself. It was nothing short of the miraculous, mighty hand of God, the power of Christ Jesus and His Holy Spirit.

God has a purpose and a plan for every life. That director took me under her arm and went on to mentor me. I assisted her at the center, mentored young moms, trained volunteers, helped with fundraising, spoke at churches and various functions on the sanctity of human life, and eventually became a director of a pregnancy resource center in the town where I live. Many people and churches had come on board initially, but after a couple of years, the funding from the community to support the center waned and it closed. For a period of five years working between the two centers, there had been many young ladies who came in for classes to learn to be good mothers. There were women who decided to keep their babies and raise them, and those who needed healing from previous abortions who came in for Post Abortion Recovery classes, and others who wanted to know Jesus on a more intimate level. It also allowed the opportunity to lead some women to Jesus Christ as their personal Lord and Savior.

But God! During this period of time of healing and restoration from the abortions and my past, I met a man at church. He seemed like a nice fellow and quite frequently I would run into him when I would go grocery shopping. I did not shop at the same time or on the same days of the week, but it got to the point that I would peek around the corner to see if he was there, I'd make my way down the aisle, and boom, there he was. We would visit for 15 minutes to an hour, and then be on our way.

Well, one Wednesday night after Bible study, he asked if I would like to go out for ice cream. I accepted and after ice cream we took a lovely walk that early July evening. I guess "fireworks" would be an understatement when we said good night, but they were literally going off in the air, and my heart was a "little" aflutter. We courted for three years, were engaged for one year, and married shortly after four years of that first date. We kid each other and periodically tell each other "You knew what you were getting into before we got married and you certainly had time to run."

Even though we both were and are what we refer to as "full on-board believers in Jesus Christ," we both had pain from past relationships. After two years of marriage, we attended a service where Bob Walker was ministering prayer for the people who were present at this gathering. Bob looked into my eyes and said "Hmmm." He then shared with us about The Jonathan House Ministries and the importance of being set free from the bondage of the past. Praise God that while we were yet sinners, God loved us in that He sent His Son, Jesus, who came to set all sinners free and we, who are in

Christ Jesus, are no longer captive to sin. There truly is freedom through the deliverance ministry. Thank you Bob and Betty!

Well, that initial meeting was back in 2008 and after both of us went through deliverance our lives have been so much freer. My husband and I have assisted the Jonathan House with editing their teaching materials, devotionals, helping at seminars, and learning deliverance ministry through assisting in the sessions. Our freedom through deliverance has been priceless. The training in deliverance and seeing people set free from bondage through ministering is as a pearl of great value. When looking around at the people in this world and recognizing how many people are walking in bondage, it just amazes me. Knowing what Jesus Christ can do for the unbeliever once they make that free will choice of choosing Him as their Lord and Savior is pivotal to their life. While the brothers and sisters in Christ need to realize that they are no longer in shackles, but free to attain all that Jesus has obtained for them is truly a treasure of an insurmountable value. That is the value of deliverance in that freedom is obtainable through The Jonathan House Ministries. With God all things are possible!

And do you know what? God is not done with any of us yet. He is not done with you, and He's not done with me. I have no idea for certain where God is taking my husband and me, but I do know that we are both willing to go wherever He decides to send us. Each of us has work to do for the advancement of the kingdom of God, and truly he whom the Son sets free, is free indeed.

The pain of my past has become like talking about a woman I used to know. The love and peace and joy that I experience as the woman I am now is quite different from the person I was way back then.

With much love and praise due you,
Thank you Father God!
Thank you Lord Jesus!
Thank you dear Holy Spirit!

Kathy Pouk, Co-editor for
The Jonathan House Ministries

Abortion Facts

Abortion is known to bring emotional torment in its aftermath, yet few understand this as being demonic and spiritual bondage. Abortion, as far as the Bible is concerned, is nothing less than the murder of an innocent person which God has created, and is a source for great spiritual bondage.[6]

What abortion clinics don't want you to know... The Silent Scream

Fetus' have feelings... as we can see in Luke 1:44, John the Baptist leaped for joy when he heard Mary's voice. During an abortion, it is true that the fetus can feel the pain and reacts to the danger. The silent scream is where a baby is being killed, and the child expresses unspeakable terror just moments before being killed. Since the Silent Scream is a subject all in itself, I am going to point you to a website, where they go into much more detail on the Silent Scream, and even show a video of an abortion in action where you can clearly see the Silent Scream taking place... a word of warning, this film is very graphic and not recommended for children to view! After all, abortion is not a pretty scene, and is nothing short of gruesome murder of an innocent and helpless child! For more information on The Silent Scream go to the website www.silentscream.org[6]

Baby Facts

Nine months (33 to 40 weeks) from conception, the baby gains about one-half pound per week as she/he prepares for birth. The bones in the child's head are soft and flexible to more easily mold for the journey down the birth canal. At 9 months (33 to 40 weeks), the unborn baby triggers labor and birth occurs, an average of 264 to 270 days after conception. Of the 45 generations of cell divisions before adulthood, 41 have already taken place. Only four more come before adolescence. Ninety percent of a person's development happens in the womb affirms ProLife Across America.[1]

Abortion's aftermath is proof alone that abortion is indeed spiritual! Jesus made it clear that murder is a source of spiritual defilement:

Matthew 15:18-20, "But those things which proceed out of the mouth come forth from the heart; and they defile the man. For out of the heart proceed evil thoughts, murders, adulteries, fornications, thefts, false witness, blasphemies: These are the things which defile a man..." [6]

Some women may not seem to be tormented so badly by abortion's aftermath, but that is if their conscience has been seared as by a hot branding iron:

1 Timothy 4:2, "Speaking lies in hypocrisy; having their conscience seared with a hot iron." [6]

The truth is that abortion is a source of enormous spiritual and mental bondage and torment. It is a means for spiritual defilement, just as cold-blooded murder is, and opens a person up for unclean spirits (demons) to enter and harass the person. Studies have shown that abortion is also linked to suicide because of such torment and bondage. Many women feel it's better that they weren't even born if they have to face such torment. Nobody knows what it's like to be in bondage, until they are the ones facing it in their own lives, and the sad truth is that many women today don't realize what they are getting themselves into until it is too late, and the damage is already done.[6]

Women who have had abortions are almost always said to experience some or many of the following symptoms:
- Bondage to shame and guilt
- Nightmares relating to the abortion
- Feeling that God would never forgive them
- Depression which can lead to suicide (Studies show that abortion is linked to suicide)
- Self-hatred for allowing themselves to do such a thing
- Sleep disorders – finding it hard to get to sleep at night
- Flashbacks and even hearing sounds of children crying
- Desire to have another baby to replace the aborted baby
- Inability to form a true loving bond with her other children
- And many, many, more...[6]

The list of side effects from an abortion is long. Jesus made it clear that murder is a means for defilement, and defilement is an open door to unclean spirits to come in and play havoc in a person's life. I believe behind almost every (if not every) case of suicide, is a spirit... a demon that drives the person to take their own life to end the pain they are facing. People who have come close to suicide will often admit that there was a force that was 'driving' them to take their own life. It often tells them that they could end all of their problems by pulling the plug.[6]

Who is behind the pro-choice movement?

The Bible tells us, we do not wage war against flesh and blood, but against various ranks of evil spirits (demons):

Ephesians 6:12, "For we wrestle not against flesh and blood, but against principalities, against powers, against the rulers of the darkness of this world, against spiritual wickedness in high places." [6]

Those who have had a decent amount of experience in the ministry of deliverance usually have come across quite a few spirits that go by the name Jezebel. The Jezebel spirits are what was behind the evil queen in the Bible which went by the name Jezebel, and are alive and well in many women today. Jezebel is accurately said to be Satan's woman. I personally believe that the women's rights movement is fueled by ruling spirits of Jezebel. The goal of

Jezebel is to usurp the woman's authority over the man in the household. The spirit of Jezebel is said to be known as 'extreme selfishness', and is the cause of many working mothers today, which can afford to stay at home with their children, but refuse to do so for the sole purpose of driving a better car and living in a better home. This same spirit tells America that the unborn child can be a hindrance to woman's rights, and that it is more important that the woman can choose to abort the hassle rather than preserving the child's life.[6]

Let me ask you this, if abortion is the murdering of innocent children (which it is!), then would you put it past "Satan's woman" to be behind such a horrific mass-killing in the world today? [6]

I didn't want to go into much detail on this (the spirit of Jezebel can be a teaching all in itself), but I did want to give you a brief understanding of the demonic force that we are up against in this battle against abortion.[6]

It is almost always necessary that such individuals go through a deliverance to rid themselves of any unclean spirits that they have picked up, tear down strongholds that have come on the scene, receive quality post-deliverance discipleship and maintain a healthy relationship with God so that they can receive and hold on to their freedom.[6]

It is also important to be sure that any bad soul ties (sex outside marriage) are broken, and the sin of fornication (or adultery) needs to be brought before the Lord in repentance as well before the deliverance process begins. After true repentance has happened and legal grounds have been broken up (bad soul ties broken, etc.), then it's time to move on to tearing down any strongholds that are present and begin casting out the spirits that have entered the person.[6]

Chapter 12
He's The Drummer

Recently, after leaving my office and computer about 9 o'clock at night, I snuggled down into my warm bed and the story of another young woman came to mind. What a blessing!

There was a 17 year old precious young woman whose family didn't teach her right ideas. As she grew into her teens, the natural circumstance happened and she became attracted to young men expecting them to fill the void in her life. She was drawn to a young black man, who she thought she was in love with. They ended up having sex and she became pregnant.

After she discovered that she was pregnant, she shared it with her mother who became very upset and told her she was to immediately have an abortion. The mother actually cursed the baby by saying it would never amount to anything, because after all, the girl was white and the boy was black. The young woman was very upset by her mother's demand and would not submit to it.

One day, she packed a few things she owned, left town, and traveled to a different state far from her mother and the home in which she had grown up. She was determined to give birth to the baby and knew it was something that she had to do.

During the process of trying to find a place to live and get a job, the Lord sent a woman into her life who led her to accept Jesus as her Lord and Savior.

At the appointed time, she gave birth to a beautiful baby boy. The moment she looked at him, she knew, without a doubt, that she had made the right choice, regardless of her mother's wishes.

This young baby, who was given life by his mother's choice to birth him, grew up, accepted the Lord, and became an extremely talented musician. He entered the music field at an early age and the Lord expanded his calling.

A spotlight shone on the drummer sitting in the front row of his church, and they explained that he not only plays instruments, but has written lots of music for God's people.

After hearing such a story, it was such a blessing to see him in person; this man who as a baby was saved from abortion, was now fulfilling the purpose that God had ordained for his life!

Thank you, Lord, for leading his mother, as a 17 year old girl, to save her child. Although the baby was conceived out of wedlock, for her to choose life was surely Your plan. While this baby was a group of cells in her body, he had a spirit and was brought forth for Your plan to bring great music to Your people!

Luke 1:41 reminds us of life within the womb: *"And it happened, when Elizabeth heard the greeting of Mary, that the babe leaped in her womb; and Elizabeth was filled with the Holy Spirit."*

God's presence in your life breaks the chains of sin. He gives you a new heart. The burden of sin lifts and joy comes. The Father's love brings restoration.[7]

You have believed lies and they warp your self-image. We are created for love. Jesus died to restore you to intimacy.[7]

"God is love, and you were created for love, to experience intimacy with your heavenly Father and with your fellow human beings." [7]

"True repentance involves both a change of heart and a change in actions." [7]

I pray you will experience Father God's affectionate embrace, feel His unconditional acceptance, and hear His tender words of love in deeper ways than you have even known. I pray you will hear His words for you: "Child, you are the one I love, and on you My favor rests." [7]

Jesus' words and actions demonstrate who the Father is and what He is like. Jesus spent 3 years demonstrating His Father's heart of compassion as He forgave sinners, healed the sick and raised the dead.[7]

Jesus is the image of the invisible God and the exact representation of God's nature… He is love. So everything He does is out of His love for us. Even when we sin, Our Father still loves us. He wants us to run to Him for comfort and forgiveness. His perfect love casts out fear. God's heart is loving and compassionate.[7]

There is nothing you can do to cause God to love you any more than He does right now. His unconditional love is based upon the loving nature of the one giving it – Him! [7]

When Adam and Eve sinned in the garden, they became ashamed, made themselves coverings and hid from God. They used fig leaves to cover themselves – to hide their sin from God. Today we use 'spiritual' fig leaves (like hyper-religious activity) to cover ourselves. These can be expressed in the acrostic FIG LEAF: [7]

F ear
I nsecurity
G uilt

L oneliness
E scapism
A nxiety
F ailure

When Christians fail, they begin to experience *fear*...
When these fears take root in their hearts, they often
become *insecure*... *Guilt* is the natural consequence of
unconfessed sin... Not being at home in God's love brings
a sense of *loneliness* and isolation... which may cause us to
turn to *escapism* (seeking comfort wherever it can be found
– often in addictions.)... Our lifestyle becomes one of
anxiety... These consequences of sin create a vicious cycle,
causing further *failure* to take place.[7]

On Facebook in June 2015, the following conversation occurred:

> "You are free to choose but you are not free from the conscquence of your choice."

> "Think really hard before you make a choice because you are going to have to live with it for the rest of your life."

> "You have a choice, no one promised that you would make the right one."

> "Too many people cannot grasp this concept."

> "Yes, it is true we suffer consequences for our actions and choices. When we repent, God knows your heart. Things can turn around. God always gives us an opportunity to find a way out."

> "Sometimes we pay consequences because of someone else's mistakes and it's not fair, but even then, God is still in control and He can turn anything into something good."

Then one woman who thinks it's not a baby, displayed anger toward all the people who were just sharing that they know we pay a consequence.

Chapter 13
Healing and Deliverance

Since we have been in the healing and deliverance ministry, we have learned much about these situations and know that many very serious physical problems can come from the emotional issues that people have experienced in years past – especially if those issues are buried and not brought forward. People need to express their feelings and forgive – especially themselves – and deal with any and all of those issues. We have seen many people with serious health issues because they have allowed sinful issues in them or their families and have not dealt with them properly. I could write a book on that alone! Our God is there for all of us, but we have to be willing to come to Him and confess, repent, and forgive. Then we must move forward in His way of life. The life that He has for His people!

Unfortunately, people believe that after they commit a sin, such as abortion, they can stuff that issue down in their mind and not talk about it or share it with anyone, possibly not even God! (Of course, He knows everything we do and think.) They live for years with those issues hidden from their family and loved ones and really themselves. As God has designed our human bodies, we will suffer very dramatically physically, emotionally, and spiritually if we choose to not confront the sin issues in our lives. It is so very important that these things be brought forth to the proper people and especially to the Lord, and then to receive God's forgiveness and healing and move ahead with Him as He directs. At The Jonathan House, we have ministered with many people who have gone through these issues, and as a result we have witnessed dramatic spiritual, emotional, and physical healings transpire.

If you know someone, or have a family member, who fits these descriptions I have just communicated, please pray with them and encourage them to receive God's healing and deliverance and progress in their Christian walk to be the person who God has designed them to be for His Kingdom!

Scripture is very clear in the fact that if you obey God, then you will be blessed, and if you disobey the Lord, you and your descendants will suffer. All over the world, people are suffering as a result of the things their ancestors did. And as you have now have learned, sin reaches back three to ten generations and we know little to nothing about our ancestors or their actions. The Bible does seem to make one distinction when it comes to the number of generations a sin can follow a family line, and that is in regard to sexual sin. Deuteronomy 23:2-3 says, *"No one born of a forbidden marriage nor any of his descendants may enter the assembly of the LORD, even down to the tenth generation. No Ammonite or Moabite or any of his descendants may enter the assembly of the LORD, even down to the tenth generation."*

Due to sin, our blessings tend to be mixed in with curses from our ancestors. Every one of us, by virtue of being born, has inherited family blessings and curses. Thankfully, the blood of Jesus provides a way to effectively deal with and remove the family curses which have been generationally passed down.

"You shall not make for yourself an image in the form of anything in heaven above or on the earth beneath or in the waters below. You shall not bow down to them or worship them; for I, the LORD your God, am a jealous God, punishing the children for the sin of the parents to the third and fourth generation of those who hate me, but showing love to a thousand generations of those who love me and keep my commandments. Exodus 20:4-6.

Regrettably, many families today are plagued with generational curses and many don't even know it. But don't forget that God is relentlessly good!

In his message "Cultivating the Fruit of the Spirit" on Facebook, Graham Cooke says it this way, "God loves faithfulness so much that even if you are being faithless to Him, He will still be faithful to you. He cannot deny Himself."

To Keep or Not To Keep

Chapter 14
Living in Freedom

Change. If you are talking about the dollars and coins you get back from a purchase, that's a good thing for most of us. If you are talking about the events that will cause you to learn a different way of thinking, a different way of doing something, or a different way to handle issues, that kind of change strikes fear in the hearts of many. Change is something that is difficult for some, even if the benefits are rewarding. Change is a part of the Kingdom of God. While God's attributes and nature never change, there are seasons of growth we experience in God which promote change.

Living in freedom is the goal of deliverance ministry. Yet, you must learn how to be constantly vigilant in preserving your freedom. The devil is a skilled enemy, lurking in the shadows, waiting for an opportunity to move in and regain ground he lost during the deliverance ministry session. Following their deliverance session at The Jonathan House, clients are given a copy of *Living in Freedom* that is a short booklet designed to give tips, advice, and encouragement to them as they continue to walk in their newfound freedom.

Many people have lived for decades with their pain and brokenness, resulting in unhealthy coping mechanisms. Evil spirits can be cast out, but bad habits have to be done away with and new habits need to be formed. While deliverance ministry can deal with the spiritual influences in your life, it is YOUR responsibility to create good habits.

Living in Freedom is designed to get you started in creating healthy habits. Change happens in stages. It's a slow process and takes place over time. At first the temptation is overwhelming to revert back to your old ways of dealing with issues and coping with life, but as you implement the suggested changes in *Living in Freedom* you will find freedom as a lifestyle can be a reality for you. In Christ you are a NEW creation, not just a polished up, refurbished model. You are brand new! Along with being brand new comes the need to learn to think differently, act differently, and respond differently. All of this takes time, but it is possible!

It is our recommendation to make *Living in Freedom* a regular part of your day for a season. Read it through weekly. Read it right when you get up, on your lunch break, or before you go to bed. You don't have to read the entire booklet through every day, but every day read over a portion of it and incorporate it into your life. As you begin to allow God to move in your life, you will see the positive changes you desire, and the temptation to revert back to your former way of life will lessen over time. While *Living in Freedom* does not address every issue you may face, it does give you tools to fight the enemy and win. Utilize *Living in Freedom* and your life will be a testament to the world of the power of Jesus Christ.

It is the heartbeat of The Jonathan House Ministries to awaken destiny in the hearts of men and women. Through deliverance, inner healing, counseling, mentoring, and discipleship, The Jonathan House Ministries is helping equip the army of God to be confident and well-equipped for the battle that rages today. The Jonathan House is committed to change the spiritual climate of America through changing the lives of people; one individual at a time.

Ungodly spirits have access to our lives by:
1. Being born; Adam and Eve's original sin.
2. Sins of generations past; Generational sin.
3. Victimization.
4. Trauma and accidents.

Everyone born on this earth has certain things they can control and certain things they have no control over. We have no control over the sin nature we are born with, and everyone struggles with it. Everything we choose to do, or not to do, has consequences. If we choose to give in to our sin nature and do something that is sinful, the devil will be there to take advantage of it and gain a foothold in our life.

None of us were able to choose our parents or our family lines. Some of us were born into family lines who have served the Lord for years, and some of us are the only Christian in our entire family. Just like we can't control the family into which we were born, neither can we control the generational curses and blessings that follow us. We all have baggage from our family lines just from being born on this earth.

The problem is further compounded when you realize the personal sins of your parents will be part of the generational sin you have to deal with, and your personal sins will be part of the generational sin your children will have to deal with. For many people, this cycle goes unnoticed and unchanged for years, resulting in entire families forfeiting their rightful place of power and authority in this earth in exchange for captivity and imprisonment.

For many people, because of being victimized, their past is riddled with painful memories of neglect, abuse, abandonment, and rejection. For those who have walked this painful road, the scars can last a lifetime if not dealt with properly. For many, these experiences happened during their childhood when they were vulnerable and had no way of protecting themselves. Childhood wounds can be inflicted on a person through mental, emotional, physical, and sexual abuses being committed against a person.

The last category for the devil to gain a foothold in an individual's life is through accidents and traumas which most commonly take place through experiencing an accident, witnessing a horrific event, or a near death experience.

Chapter 15
Experience God's Love

You need to come to your right senses. You need to confess and repent of your sin, and forgive yourself and others. See God as your source of love. Anticipate His compassion. And, return to His presence.

The love of God is a gift. It is free and undeserved. There is nothing you can do to be more loved or less loved. His love is unconditional. His love brings healing.

Our anger, fear, and distrust – which are often rooted in our hidden core pain – easily spill over into our marriage, family, career, ministries, and our walk with God, and the effects greatly hinder our lives. What are the strongholds (destructive habits or patterns of thinking) that might be holding you back? What are your hidden issues? God wants to touch your heart and emotions. He wants to restore healthy emotions in your relationships.

Dwelling in a place where God's love is constantly renewing and restoring you to intimacy with others can take place only when you are willing to walk in the light of God's love. The very purpose of Light is to set us free from anything that hinders deeper intimacy with Him. Darkness is a moral state where you hide things, have secrets, and give the enemy ground to traffic in your life. The very thing the enemy wants to take from us is the very thing he lost – intimacy and fellowship with God. Darkness gives the enemy access to operate in your life. Light is rooted in humility – a willingness to be known for who we really are. Freedom begins with a simple willingness to walk in the light.

The father of lies wants you to be deceived and believe lies about yourself. Confessing to others a past area of sin in your life becomes a catalyst to prevent you from ever committing that sin again. Confessing releases a deeper cleansing and freedom from sins. God brings that new level of freedom to you!

We have witnessed wonderful healings, both emotional and physical, during or soon after they have gone through deliverance. During the process of deliverance, they confess, repent and forgive themselves and others, and receive freedom and healing from God. Following their session, we teach them how to walk in their new-found freedom!

God wants you filled with truth, love, and grace. He wants you to rule over strongholds. He wants everything to be changed and realigned with the kingdom of heaven – your attitudes, your desires, and your motivation so that you are free. You are to walk in humility and repentance.

End Notes

[1]ProLife Across America, Mary Ann Kuharski, Director

[2]© 2015 Merriam-Webster, Incorporated

[3]Peter J. Horrobin, Founder Ellel Ministries, LaGrange, England, "Healing through Deliverance, Volume 2" ©1991, 2003

[4]Mike Huckabee, Governor (on Facebook, 2015)

[5]World Health Organization (WHO) – Statistics by the World Health Organization

[6]© 2003-2008 Robert L. Boldt, www.GreatBibleStudy.com

[7]Jack Frost, author, "Experiencing Father's Embrace" ©2002

Book Orders

To order additional copies of
To Keep or Not To Keep as gifts for friends,
family, co-workers, pastors or your church library,
call (507) 282-8845.

Other books available by
The Jonathan House Ministries:

- Food From the King's Table

- Freedom Through Healing and Deliverance

- God's Flower Garden

- Living in Freedom

- Sonship – Walking in Our Royal Calling

- Trust Me, Child!

Other Resources Available

❖ E-devotional

"Food from the King's Table" is a free weekly devotional provided by The Jonathan House Ministries. To start receiving our devotional, either E-mail us at info@jonathanhouseministries.com or visit our website www.jonathanhouseministries.com

❖ Freedom Through Healing and Deliverance DVD Teaching Series

Freedom Through Healing and Deliverance is a seven-part teaching series that introduces the viewer to the ministry of healing and deliverance. This teaching series is great for those wanting to know more about the ministry of healing and deliverance. Filled with biblical teaching, great insights, and practical real-world examples, this teaching series is a must have for every church library.

❖ Sonship: Walking In Our Royal Calling DVD Teaching Series

Sonship: Walking In Our Royal Calling is an eight-part teaching series designed to call forth destiny. Each lesson deals with particular topics that hold people back from truly becoming a mighty warrior in the kingdom of God. You will not be the same after viewing Sonship!

❖ Refusing to Settle: The Journey of a World-Changer CD Teaching Series

Refusing To Settle: The Journey of a World-Changer is a nine-part teaching series designed to launch you into the greater life waiting for you. You can live the greater life simply by blooming where you are planted. Dare to leave behind baseline Christianity and embrace the greater life for which you were created!

The Jonathan House Ministries

Where the Captives Go
to Be Set FREE!

www.jonathanhouseministries.com

E-mail: info@jonathanhouseministries.com

P.O. Box 5936
Rochester, MN 55903
507-282-8845